TO LOSE A PENNY

By

Savannah Lynn

To Lose A Penny
Copyright © 2022 by Savannah Lynn

All rights reserved. No part of this book may be reproduced or transmitted in any form or by any means, electronic or mechanical, including photocopying, recording, or by any information storage and retrieval system without express written permission from the author, except in the case of brief quotations embodied in critical reviews and certain other noncommercial uses permitted by copyright law.

Printed in the United States of America.

Brilliant Books Literary
137 Forest Park Lane Thomasville
North Carolina 27360 USA

Acknowledgment

△My Family, the triangle with two propellers, You all are my rock; my biggest supporters and I love you all dearly, The men who's handwriting makes up our narrators: my father, my brother, my grandpa, my mentor and my best friend, I would not be where or who I am today without any of you, Mak for being my first fangirl and giving me the skydiving idea, Brooklyn for the idea of how Lise's "meet-cute", Mark and Joseph for telling me it is called a "button up" not "button down", Everyone else who has believed in me, or challenged me, I wouldn't be the writer I am without you, Thank you all for helping make my dream a reality, I hope you enjoyed it and I can't wait for our next adventure,

Savannah Lynn (Hoelle)

Dedication

You'll see,

October 10

This is bullshit. Absolute, crazy, ridiculous, pointless bullshit. My best friend, Annalise, got me this; she wants me to write, to open up, or explore my feelings or something. She said it was either this or talking to a therapist. As if my wife dying is going to turn me into Shakespeare. Don't get me wrong, I appreciate the gesture, but it's just not me. I am a very logical person. There's no underlying secret or explanation. There's nothing to talk about. I married the love of my life, and last month she died. Penny died. By a bullet that was meant for me. Sucks. Fucking sucks, actually, but pouring my heart onto a page isn't going to fix it. Nothing I can say or do could ever bring her back. So, I've just accepted that and am learning to live with it.

But anyway, Annalise knows I won't talk to her, so I'm guessing she wants me to use this. Again, ridiculous. But I also know she's going to check if I did, so I need to make it, at least, look like I tried. Lord knows I've let enough people down, I don't want to add her to the list.

Such random words. Christmas is coming soon. I already saw some moron with lights up. Not like orange Halloween lights, straight-up red and white deck the damn hall's lights. Idiot. This is easy, I can do this. The ice cream truck just drove by, not going to lie; I wanted to run out the door like a seven-year-old with mama's cash. Emotional words. Sad. Depressed. Lonely.

Blah blah blah. This is a difficult time. I need a beer. Other random words that make sentences longer fill up the rest of the page. Alright, I think that will get her off my back. Don't expect anything else from me. Bye.

> Sincerely,
> This is Bullshit

November 12

Alright, maybe Annalise had a point. Maybe it's not such a bad idea. I mean, I can speak freely; there are no consequences or judgment. So, I've decided I'm going to write all the things I don't want to say to anyone else—random shit. Like ideas I have or rants. I want to get out my head but don't want to watch my friends' eyes glaze over like donuts. That and only that kind of thing is what I'll talk to you about. Okay, nothing personal, no feelings, and just to be extra protective, this is anonymous. No names. Well fuck, I already said Annalise and Penny. Okay, I will remain anonymous. You don't know me; I don't need to know you. Plain and simple.

Moving on to my pre-mentioned rant. Brains. I want to talk about how stupid human brains are. They remember the most random things at the most unexpected time. Like you ever walked down the street, and your brain just goes, "dude, remember what the cafeteria in 3rd grade smells like?" And then, BAM, you smell it.

Well, I had a moment like that today, but instead, it was one of my treasured memories, not some random one. You know the kind, the one you keep on a film reel, constantly playing in the back of your mind. The one you replay when you are in traffic or a doctor's lobby. I was walking along and suddenly remembered the pillows in the hotel room for Penny and our honeymoon. They were these awful mustard yellow that had the texture of the ugly shag carpet from the 60s. The dingy feather sacks that every grandmother in America still has on her couch.

Penny and I made a joke that it felt like our grandmothers put cameras in them and were spying on us. We tumbled over on the floor at the idea of our grandmas in an FBI van with a headset and flashing monitors. We laughed and laughed until we honeymooned. And we somehow convinced ourselves it was true. So, needless to say, the puke pillows spent the night in the bathtub.

I hadn't thought of those pillows in years. It made me smile, and I instinctively pulled out my phone to call Penny.

And that's why brains are stupid. It can remember the exact feel and color of pillows I saw one time, but it can't remember that my wife is dead.

Another stupid thing about brains is how they explicitly remember the bad moments, but you have to really focus on remembering the good ones.

I can barely remember coming home from overseas. I can barely remember the day my little brother was born. I don't remember my wedding day at all. It was a total blur; I was so nervous that I couldn't have told you what band played or what our colors were. I remember our vows; I remember her, and I remember the sunflowers everywhere. That's it.

But yet I remember the paisley scrubs of the nurse who held my hand when I broke my arm in 7th grade. I remember way too many things from deployment. I remember the exact curvy line artwork in the funeral home where we buried my uncle. To the point, you could put a paper in front of me, and I could draw it.

Am I crazy? Is it just me, or do you feel that way too? I'm willing to bet if I asked you what your worst memory was, it's probably something along the lines of "when ____ left" or "when ____ died" or "when ____ hurt me". And I bet you can tell me the color of the hospital wall, or the shirt you were wearing. You could probably tell me how your shoe was half untied, and you had pickle breath. For some reason, the details stick with us.

My worst memory I pretty much relive every night in my sleep. Give ya one wild guess about the worst moment of my life. Go ahead, guess.

Yep, Livingston Road. Black blazer that had a little bit of glitter still on it from a birthday party months ago. Turquoise top with a bow at the collar. Her heels were clicking on the pavement—her giggle. Our clasped hands were swinging slightly. The heat of the Chinese food against my side, the pressure of its weight on my elbow. The shine of his gun. The silver clip on the alligator skin purse he had a death grip on.

The gunshot. I've heard a million gunshots in my life, but this one sounded different; it seemed to move in slow motion. Penny's ribs were cracking like dollar store glowsticks. The entirety of her weight fell onto me. The sharp, needlelike pain in my side as the bullet found a new home. Penny being just a sideshow attraction. The hole that seemed infinite in her chest. The blood splatter constellations on her face covering her freckled ones. Her telling me to be calm, calling me love and darling no less than

50 times. The blinding sirens showed up what felt like years later. The rip of the Velcro strapping us to backboards, keeping us just out of reach except for our pointer fingers.

The doors of the ambulance slammed open. The squeak of the wheels down the hallway. Freezing. I was freezing my balls off. She turned and looked at me before they separated us. She looked up with big, brown eyes I'd built my home in, her favorite shirt dangling in shreds, her engagement ring earning it's name as a blood diamond. She took a huge breath and smiled, said the last words I'd ever hear her speak: I love you.

That moment lives rent-free in my mind. I close my eyes, sleep, breathe, and that moment is all I can feel. The heavy, scratchy blanket on my bare skin, the annoying peach pattern on the wall. The pain in my side couldn't flicker in the presence of the pain in my chest.

The day my life ended, of course, I remember every damn detail. Yet the best days, I'm left with bits and pieces.

Wow, I haven't told anyone about that last I love you. I didn't want anyone to think she suffered. It was just a more straightforward idea to live with that she didn't feel any pain. I haven't told anyone the truth. I sure opened up to you quickly, didn't I? Yikes. Well, as I said, it might not be a bad thing. We will see, I guess. But anyway, that wasn't my point; my point is brains are stupid.

Sincerely,
Bitch Brain

November 20

Surprise. Me again. I didn't think I'd ever write to you again, honestly, but something happened today, and I can't really tell anyone else. So lucky you, get to hear all about it. I ran into my ex, Natayla. I was just grabbing a bagel at that place on 3rd, and there she was. She looked so different I almost didn't recognize her; it wasn't until she was hugged around me and her perfume reached my nose that I knew, for sure.

Her blonde hair was now an icy silver. She had some fancy leather sports coat, fur-lined gloves, and high heels. She was always in heels; I swear if they made high-heeled slippers, she would wear them with pajamas. She looked slightly older, which was understandable; it's been 9 years.

She was so happy to see me, she practically pulled me to a table and started rapidly firing the normal "how you been" questions. I usually hate these situations; it's always awkward. Like you go from seeing someone naked, spilling your heart, withholding no secrets, picturing futures with them to not being able to talk about the weather.

But this was different. This was like slipping into an old, broken pair of sneakers, comfortable and familiar.

She asked me if I was seeing anyone; I paused. I wasn't sure I wanted to get into the whole story of Penny. But then I felt guilty for not mentioning her. So, I just said I was a widower and prayed she wouldn't pry.

But let me tell you, no one ever prepares you for that title. "Boyfriend" catches you off guard at first. Then it wraps around you like a comforter. Then "fiance," you get a warning, because well, you decide when to ask. "fiance" feels like a DMV waiting line. A stepping stone but not there yet. Then "husband" comes along, and you wear that one like your wedding ring. Always on, shiny and steady, and forever. But "widower" is getting squished into a pair of brand-new dress shoes. Two sizes too small, no socks, and you have to walk around like you aren't dying inside.

She gave me the trademark head tilt and "I'm so sorry". I could tell she wanted to know more, but my savor in an apron called out her order number. I walked up to the counter with her; she picked up a blueberry muffin and a large coffee. Two creams, no sugar.

I was surprised; she hates blueberry. I called her out on it, and she simply said, "People can change." Then she gave me her card and said, we should grab a drink sometime. The bell on the door dinged with her exit before I could focus enough to answer. The dude behind the counter called out my number and then high-fived me for "scoring the hot blueberry chick's number." I walked to work in silence, with no headphones; the bustling city felt like a graveyard. The shiny windows and muffled laughs disappeared; I was left alone with only the thought of Natalya. My bitch brain kept memories of her on a loop the whole day until I finally decided to call.

Yes, I called. I am having a drink with her tomorrow. I don't know why but I feel like this is something I just need to do. I don't know what I'm expecting or where it's gonna go. But I just feel like this is one of those things I'll regret not doing more than doing.

Maybe this is a fate thing; and maybe this is a stupid thing. I don't know. But me having no idea what's going on or feeling like myself isn't a newsflash. I don't fucking know anything, but I think I need to do this, and anyone else would kill me if I told them.

Sincerely,
Again, Lucky You

November 22

First dates are always so weird. It feels like you are on a tightrope. Balancing between showing enough of yourself to seem open but holding back enough to not seem overeager. That "magical" first part of a relationship has always been so fascinating to me. The part where your partner only seems to carry about the positive things, where you are from, your occupation, your pet's names. They cling to those little things until the inevitable happens, something slips out. Divorce. Alcohol problem. Lives with their mother. Good friends with your mortal enemy. After that, it's like the first hit in Battleship; they get obsessed with that red pin high and keep searching.

Penny and I used to talk about this all the time; humans are awful. We get so worried about protecting ourselves; we shift our focus to finding flaws in them that we dig deep enough until we find one. We manifest our own ending by looking for it. It's like we are so terrified to get accidentally broken, we break ourselves first. As if a clean-cut knife slice hurts less than jagged stabs.

It was so funny to Penny and I because relationships are the only thing we do that with. We don't walk out of a movie theater because we are scared of the movie's ending. We have one bad day at work, but we don't quit our whole job. But that's exactly what we do with people. We see a red flag as a checkered one, game over. Unless we already love them, then we ignore the red flags. We ignore all the flags, which can be just as bad.

Anyway, way off-topic; that's why I hate first dates. I went out with Nat tonight, and it wasn't like that at all. Because that wasn't our first date, there was no awkward audition to play the role of myself. She already knows me. She didn't ask me where I was from; she asked me how my parents were doing in Carolina. She asked me about work. She didn't ask about Lucy, my golden retriever but to be fair; she didn't know she existed. Luce is Penny and my dog. Well, "and my" is a stretch; she is Penny's dog. She tolerated me.

My point is, it was so easy with Natalya. I wish every first date I ever had could be that easy. I wish it was socially acceptable to just make a cheat sheet of yourself and then hand it to your date. Like

From: North Carolina
Age: 33
Job: Admin at an architecture firm
Family: Juliet (mom) + Edward (dad)
Happy, helpful, don't like talking about sad things
Sarah (sister, 5 years older)
Married, two kids, Lindsey and Jacob
Michael (brother, 14 years younger)
Little punk but a good kid
Likes: Arizona Coyotes, chocolate ice cream, tattoos, American shit
Dislikes: olives, traffic, couples that sit on the same side of a booth, sushi, idiots, slow walkers

Hot buttons: politics (you believe and vote for what you want, I'll do the same), open mouth chewers.

See? Easy. Why can't I just print this out and hand it to every person I meet and be like, alright, are you even going to be worth my time?

Well, Nat knew this sheet, had it fucking memorized. We talked and caught up for what felt like hours. It was perfect, almost until she reached my hand and started teasing me about showing up to date with paint on my hand.

Her facial expression quickly changed when she realized the blue splotch on my ring finger was a tattoo, not a stain.

"It's a long story," was my reply. That's been my reply to a lot of things lately, a coverall band-aid that eliminates any situation. I just didn't want to tell her, at least not yet. That tattoo has an intimate story that very few people knew. I didn't want to open up that quickly.

Later on, I walked her to her car. I just wanted to make sure she was safe, we had dinner in the city, and it can be a little scary at night. It was a completely innocent intention, but then she grabbed my shirt and pulled me on top of her. I pulled back before our lips met. I wasn't ready for that; I can't, I just can't even think about kissing anyone. She protested, of course, saying we used to not even make it to the car, especially in a dress like that.

It was true; she did look good. She had on a black velvet bodycon dress. Don't judge me; Penny taught me that word. Her silver hair was half up in a clip, the rest of it draping over her shoulders. She had on her "sun" necklace. I say "sun" because to me; it looks like a spider. What kind of sun is black? She had on grey eye makeup and bright red lipstick that 9 years ago would have been smeared all over me.

But I couldn't; it wasn't physically a possibility in my mind. It felt like a time warp. A glitch in the matrix. Like we suddenly arrived at a different future that was meant to be all along. I didn't like it. I still don't. I feel cheated like this was the second-place trophy, and the first place one is in a coffin that I spent 20 mins deciding the interior. The correct way, the way it was meant to be, was hinged in that box, wrapped around it, and buried deeper than my fingers can dig. I felt that running into Nat was an apology cookie from God. A band-aid for the whoopsie. But I don't want a band-aid; I want my wife. I tried to play it cool, it's not Nat's fault, but I'm sure she could tell something was up.

I just don't know what to think now. Do I accept the cookie, or do I go sulk in misery for the next 50 years? Because building a house of sorrow doesn't sound like a good life, but it also feels like if I accept the apology cookie, it feels like I am okay with the whoopsie. I'm not. Not at all. I want her back. I'd trade Nat or every woman on the planet and my own right arm to have that woman back. I just don't know what to do. Help me. And as for the tightropes of first dates, this is me:

Sincerely,
An Artistic Genius

November 30

Do you believe in signs? Like little hints in life that God or the universe or whatever gives you along the way? Well, I don't really; Penny always did. She was big into that stuff. She read her horoscope every morning. She left jars full of random weeds and rocks all around the place. She'd burn some sage stick every bad day to get rid of "hoocha." She constantly looked for signs, and most of the time, she got them. She always lived on the edge, like her soul was permanently in a flowy dress, on the edge of a cliff, delicately dancing with disaster. She was the dreamer of the relationship. I envied her for it; I was the planner, the every-minute-scheduled-pros-and-cons-list-on-a-yellow-legal-pad type. But not her; she would make huge decisions on the winds of fate. I mean, the woman literally decided a marriage proposal with the flip of a coin. Luckily that wasn't my proposal; that was long before me. Remind me, I'll tell you that story sometime.

Anyway, I always half-ass believed in that shit. But Natalya and I were talking about the next step. Bleh, I sounded like a teenage girl about to get kissed under the bleachers before homeroom. Gross. No. Okay, sex. Bang. Fuck. We've kissed a few times now, which I'm still not entirely comfortable with, but she was so sweet and understanding. I felt like I kinda owed it to her. And I was hoping that would be enough, but it wasn't. She immediately started pushing it, steadily dragging me towards a line I wasn't ready to cross.

But I was honestly stumped on the whole thing; I tried to look at it logically. I mean, on the one hand: sex is good. On the other: I feel like it would just somehow erase the past 8 years of my life. Like Penny and our life together would disappear Marty McFly style. Which is crazy; I know Penny is still a part of me; she always will be.

All thru dinner tonight, I found myself looking for signs. Not even looking, but a full-on exploration expedition. I overanalyzed every word said, every move made. Looked for 1111 on the checkout receipt; Penny always said if you see that number, it's meant to be. I looked at the traffic lights. I urban dictionaried our waitress's name. Every single thing I could think of to make this decision for me. But the check didn't have a single 1 on it. The traffic lights flashed yellow. Violet is just a purple flower. And my gut feelings were silent. I wrestled with this all night; I'm sure it was an awful date for her. I wasn't very talkative or interesting. I was just about to give up, but we got to my truck, and there was a flyer on the windshield.

NO MONEY DOWN BLOWOUT SALE!

It was an ad from the car dealership around the corner. After the initial insult of someone feeling the need to put this on my perfectly fine truck, I realized how it was folded. The only word showing was "NO." My heart leaped into my throat. I had spent all night looking for signs, and now that it's here in front of me, I didn't know what to think.

What do you think? That's definitely a sign, right? I mean a straight-up NO right on my dash. That's gotta be one, right?

Regardless, it gave me enough gumption to tell her I wasn't ready. She tried to put on an understanding face, but I could tell she wasn't happy. To be completely honest, I wasn't happy about it either. I knew it's the right thing to do, but I felt emasculated somehow.

It's like I know I could do it. And Nat isn't exactly new territory, but being a widower is. And I am no fucking good at it. I hate it. If you asked me a year ago of all your loved ones whose death would hurt the most? I wouldn't have been able to answer. Too tough of choice. You know? It's impossible to categorize. I'm sure you've got different loves for different people; their losses would be different too. I've been asked that before, and I never knew the answer. But now I know. And I am being forced to live it. And as if losing her wasn't enough, I feel like I am losing me too. I mean, this is not me at all. I'm a fucking man. I'm the kind to throw a woman onto a bed or truck seat or whatever and take her over in the exact way she wants me to. That's me. Not this undecided, feeling, mushy shit. Like I said, I feel like a teenage girl. Clearly, I'm struggling with the whole thing, but I guess we will see what happens.

Sincerely,
Gotta Go Pick
Out a Prom Dress

December 1

    I did what I thought was the right thing. I told Annalise everything about Nat, the signs, my doubts, and fears, all of it. I ripped a hole in my chest and poured everything on the pizza shop's tablecloth. I love that after all these years, she and I are still best friends. There is nothing off-limits when it comes to us. I always get so nervous when I tell her I'm seeing someone because it's never the same reaction twice. Sometimes the girlfriend would get territorial and jealous and put a strain on Annalise and I. Sometimes; they would just be disgustingly affectionate to me and overly fake nice to her.

    Only with Penny was it normal; they met like two adult human beings and got along. She respected the closeness of our friendship and then created one of their own. I will never forget the amount of joy I felt when I asked Penny who she was having lunch with, and she said Annalise for the first time. She was totally understanding and even supportive of us; she used some Grey's Anatomy references. Something like "she can be your Christina as long as I'm still McDreamy" something like that. I don't know, I've only ever watched like two episodes, but if that's how Penny made sense of it, who was I to stop her.

    My boys were always jealous of me being able to have both. Not that I got to be with both of them or anything, but I always had an outside woman's opinion, and Penny always had a woman who's dealt with me for a decade's opinion. It helped us thru quite a bit throughout the years. I didn't have to worry about either of them getting angry or possessive. And since I told both of them everything, I didn't worry about secrets coming out. Well, that's not entirely true; I did worry a few times about big presents or surprise parties because Lise can't keep a secret to save her life. But other than that, I had nothing to worry about.

Until now, because everything has gone to hell, and I have to tell my only living best friend that I'm seeing the woman she once called "Satan's Whore Incarnated."

She kinda just froze; she stopped twirling the curl I know she leaves out of her hair tie for when she gets nervous. She took her glasses off and pinched the bridge of her nose, staring at the tablecloth, refusing to meet my eyes. Then when she finally looked up, she kicked my knee under the table, not with full force but enough that it stung a bit.

"Are you fucking kidding me?" was her long-awaited response. Then she launched into a tailwind of the greatest hits of our relationship. All the bad things Nat did last time we were together. She brought up the constant phone tracking, the office party that ended in a screaming match in front of my boss. Her pretending to be my wife so she could burn my mail.

I had heard this album before. I had these tunes memorized, and I had an excuse for just about all of them, until she pulled the lowest card she could play. She mentioned the night I told her never to speak of.

I feel like in order to get the whole picture of this situation; I need to tell you that story too. I don't like talking about it, though. The only people that know about it are Annalise and Penny, but even Pen just got the summary. But like I said, you need the whole picture.

So, when Natalya and I were dating all those years ago, we got in a fight. Well, we got in a lot of fights, but this one was different. It ended with her storming out and me calling Annalise to take me to the hospital at 2 o'clock in the morning.

I'll never forget the look on her face when she walked in and found me covered in blood, the carpet littered with broken glass and ripped pictures. Her eyes quickly swirled with confusion and fear as my throbbing ankle and dislocated shoulder answered the question she didn't need to ask. Her eyes looked very different than Nat's had looked earlier. Her baby blues went icy, cold, evil, and crazy. They didn't look human, and they were inescapable. She, by every definition, snapped. She pushed me down the stairs; she threw wine glasses and picture frames at me. And as if she knew she was going to pick this fight, she wedged the doors shut from the outside. I was trapped in her tornado of fury over some Instagram-like or some shit.

That's when I finally saw what Annalise had been seeing all along. I begged her to go along with the lie I told the doctors, and she agreed if I would end things with Nat. I said I would, but then I came home to a clean house, fluffed pillows, and homemade soup, and an apology. I forgave her, but Annalise didn't forgive me. She said she didn't like the man I was with Nat and that she loved me too much to watch me get destroyed. So, she left. I didn't see her for about 9 months, the only time in our 12 years that we didn't have pretty much daily contact.

So, I can totally understand how me dating the only person that's ever become between us is her worst-case scenario. But to her credit, she was very level-headed and strategic. She presented logical arguments and backed them with facts. She didn't scream or cry or throw a fit. I was on the fence, truly, until she said something that hit me so hard, I memorized every word:

"Honestly, Penny was the master of the whole universe thing. But I believe in energy and the concept of Karma. Whatever you put out, you get back. And yeah, you can ask for signs and hold crystals and light candles and keep lucky rainwater in your shower. (Yes, Penny did that) But at the end of the day, you're only going to attract the signs you want to see. Which means on some level, deep down, you already knew the answer."

When she said that, it hit like a lightning bolt. I mean it HIT. I felt it shiver down my spine; I felt that truth crash onto me like a thunderstorm. It has always been a no; I didn't need the universe to tell me that. She was a no before Penny; why the hell would she be a yes now? I guess things are just harder to see clearly when they are standing right in front of you. When all the nostalgia for a preserved past hit, just to realize the memory has been tainted. I know what I have to do. Annalise just confirmed it. I'm so thankful I have her to talk this shit out with.

                    Sincerely,
                    It's A No From Me Dawg

December 2

    Okay, although it's not entirely clear where you stand on the whole Natalya thing, I'm pretty sure you are going to be mad at me. I've decided to give her another chance despite Annalise's aggressive recommendation. I was thinking; people change; I'm not the same person I was 8 years ago, so maybe neither is she. And I owe it to myself to at least see if she has changed. I think she could be good for me if she has. She has been so sweet and understanding of this whole taking-it slow thing. I don't know, I feel like this could end up being a good thing. Or even if it doesn't, and it ends horribly, maybe it will lead me to something. I don't know how to explain it. But there's just something in me, telling me this is what I'm supposed to do. This is not necessarily the right thing to do, but it's what I need to do. I don't know; I can't explain it. And maybe I should stop wasting your time saying "I don't know" over and over. So, I'll write again when I do know, at least a little bit.

                                            Sincerely,
                                     I'll Keep You Posted

December 10

Okay, maybe she hasn't changed as much as I thought. I like her; I do, and we have good times together, but she's starting to show her old self again. Constantly "requesting my location" and going thru my phone. She even opened my bank statements and asked about charges. Like what the fuck, yes, I cheated on you in a gas station and then bought a slushie. Like God damn, can't a man buy a Slim Jim in peace?

She just is starting to get a little crazy... and punchy. I mean, she's a girl, so they don't hurt too bad, but they do bruise up. And I'm kinda tired of lying to everyone. Like I told Annalise, I played a game of pickup hockey, I told the boys it was a sex injury, Told my mom over FaceTime I ran into a filing cabinet at work. Why I didn't stick to one lie, I don't know. That would have made sense. But I just get so flustered and defensive, I just spit out the first thing that comes to my mind and quickly change the subject.

But I don't have to lie to you, and I think that's why I'm even writing in the first place. Because I don't have to bullshit. I can say where the bruises came from. I can say I wish she would stop. I can say that I'm so scared of losing her and being alone again that I feel like I can't even fight back.

Before you judge me for lying, consider this: I am a man. A decently sized, 33-year-old, in my physical prime.

with years of military training, manly, man. And she is a 5'4" skinny girl with bright blue fingernails. So, if I did tell the truth, I would hear things like "oh, did she hurt the little baby" or "get him a band-aid for his boo-boo." My size and stature completely devalue any claim I have. And I know that. And I also know that since boys are 4 years old watching superman on tv, we've had it pounded in our heads to never show weakness.

I mean, it's sad, but it's true. We, as kids, have things glued into the inside of our skulls that, even as adults, we can't ignore. For men, it's to never break, never show weakness. Emotions are bad and should be dealt with alone. Otherwise, you're a sissy. And women, oh god, don't get me started on all the bullshit media messages women have to deal with. They are told that finding love and getting married is life's only endgame. That nothing they do matters unless there's a diamond on their hand when they do it. They get both ends of the shit stick; they want to be an entrepreneur and take on the business world, they are seen as cold, heartless, unnatural for ignoring their motherhood instincts. They want to do nothing but be a stay-at-home mom; they are anti-feminist because how dare you sit at home when thousands of women have fought for you to have the right to work? Dude, I'm gonna reign it back in; I could write a whole damn book about that bullshit. Penny and I used to talk about it all the time.

But anyway, we live in a world where men can't show emotion and women can't do anything right. And I really just wanted to say that sucks. That fucking sucks.

So, I'll just wrap this up by saying: it hurts. It hurts to lie. The bruises hurt. Loving Nat hurts. Not knowing anything and feeling like my life is completely pointless hurts. And I fucking miss Penny.

                                      Sincerely,
                                      Which Hurts Most All

December 15

We broke up. I'll pause to let you have a mini dance party... You, along with the rest of the world.

We were good for a little bit there, hence the reason you and I haven't talked in a while. We had a few fights but nothing major. She seemed to really care, and honestly, it was nice. Lately, it feels like everyone is on eggshells around me. Even my family handles me with kid gloves, and it's hard to tell if they care because it's me, or they care because Penny died. I know it's just mind games within myself but it still gives me an uneasy feeling that I have grown to despise.

It's like Penny wasn't the only thing that died that day. My happiness, my sanity, my identity, my sense of understanding, all of it, was in that casket with her. I could practically see it lying next to her. Well, lying next to her body, she wasn't there. Even looking at her, it felt like she wasn't in the room, and I hated it. I fucking hated it. I hated the green walls of the funeral home. I hated how cold she looked. And she wasn't smiling. That bothered me the most; her smile was her trademark. She had a smile that made life worth living. Her smile was the electricity that turned the Earth. And if she was being ripped away from me, the least God could do would be to let me see her smile. But no, the mortician said it's impossible and against the policy.

Damn. Sorry, major tangent, back to Nat. So, she had practically moved herself in, And I was okay with it; it was nice sharing the space with someone again. But then she slowly started changing things. She changed the comforter on the bed to one from her place. She recorded a million episodes of some reality show on the DVR. She started buying Christmas decorations and putting them all over. She changed so many little things I didn't even notice, until she took it too far, the picture of Penny and I's wedding day in our bedroom was replaced by a picture of her and me.

That's when it clicked. The comforter she replaced was one Penny's mom gave us. She deleted Penny's cooking show to make room for her stupid Housewives of WhoTheFuckCares. She bought new decorations to not put-up Penny's. She was trying to erase her; she was trying to replace her. She was trying to revert back to 9 years ago like nothing has changed. But things have changed, and so have I.

Admittedly, I snapped. I started screaming at her. She, of course, was ready for the fight. She started to argue and pushed my shoulders back into the wall. I pushed her back. I was done, dude. I was at the end of my mother fucking rope, and I was ready to turn that rope into a noose. I was over her shit. I was over my work's shit. I was over life's shit. I'm just fucking done. And if she wanted a real fight, she'd fucking get one.

We screamed and insulted each other until we were blue in the face. She threw the picture frame at me. I said, "I'd rather spend the rest of my life alone than be with a frigid heartless bitch like you." It got ugly, fast. She raised her arm up to hit me, and I grabbed her wrist. I watched the ice in her eyes crack as she didn't know what to do next.

Then that bitch figured it out. She called, what I only can assume is an old fuck-buddy, who is a cop. Within 10 minutes, he came barging into my house, and the curtain went up on Nat's one-woman show. She started crying and lying, saying I hit her. She even, within the conversation, managed to move positions, so it looked as though I threw the frame at her. She was very good at a game I didn't even know I was playing.

I tried to tell the truth. I tossed my pride out the window, showed the bruises, the phone tracking all of it. But clearly, this man was under her magical vagina spell, and it was like talking to a wall. A wall that couldn't keep his eyes off her tits or his bottom lip out of his teeth. I didn't have a chance.

She kept spewing mascara-stained lies, and I was screwed. Eventually, he ended up agreeing not to arrest me at her recommendation and that I just had to leave for the night so Nat could get her stuff.

Can you believe that? Kicked out of my own fucking house. God only knows what I'll come home to. She'll probably destroy the place. Break all the dishes and picture frames, pour my good whiskey into the drawers of my dresser. Fuck officer fuckboy on my bed.

Luckily, they let me grab a few things before I was escorted out. I got every single picture of Penny I had, the watch my grandpa got me, and the box of mementos under my bed. All the things that are irreplaceable. Filled my bag with that and one pair of boxers and drove to Annalise's. She was furious; I had to convince her not to go, full-on murderer, which was hard to do, believe me. But yeah, so, I'm here, in 'Lise's ex's PJs drinking bourbon, wondering how bad prison for life could actually be. So yeah, it may have cost me everything that I own, but we broke up.

Sincerely,
Yay

December 17

When was the last time you sang? Like full-on, diva mode activated, pretended your life wasn't falling apart, ignoring the rest of the world, deep breath screaming lyrics, sang. Well, that happened to me today. For the first time in a long time, a very long time, I sang. Some stupid poppy boppy song, but I just let it go. I forgot everything for a minute.

But then the song ended, the real world came back. I drove back to my house; I sat in the driveway for a minute, half tempted to just leave it. Throw a for sale sign in the front yard, all furniture, clothing, and memories included.

Well, long story short, it was half destroyed. It was messy, clothes thrown all over, dishes broken, entire cans of shaving cream, cooking oil, and wine was poured on the floor and counter. It was not as bad as I thought it would be, but definitely not good.

Ha, I feel like that could be the title of my autobiography: Not As Bad As I Thought It Would Be, But Definitely Not Good. Anyway, I'm having a hard time focusing, so I guess I'll talk to you when I can think straight.

Sincerely,
A Mess

December 19

What's your happy place? Seriously take a second to think about it. Is it a sandy beach paradise? Or a cup of hot cocoa and a mountain range view? Is it mama's kitchen? Or is it the arms of a person who feels like home?

Let me give you some unwanted advice, if your happy place is a person: change it. Go swimming in the ocean at midnight. Go make snow angels. Go to Home Depot and build a house.

Seriously, make it from scratch. Make it where you know every nook and cranny, where the scuffs on the tile are only from your heel, where every chip is from your hands. Spill your secrets into the drywall and hang them as proudly as picture frames. Splatter your heart all over in uneven shades. Trust me. If your happy place has a heartbeat, build a damn house.

Otherwise, when you lose them, you'll end up like me. Jumping from happy place to happy place, one being familiar lips, the next being a bar. Then guess what, you'll lose both of those too.

The past few months, I had become a regular at this bar right up the street. I didn't go as much when Nat and I were together but still once a week or so. I got to know people there, the other regulars, the bartenders, even some of the bands. It was nice; I almost felt homey, like I belonged in some way. And last night, I ruined that too.

One of the guys and I were just talking, shooting the shit, and maybe it was the empty glasses, or maybe this was a long time coming, but he crossed a line. And I snapped. He joked about Penny, well, Penny dying. And before I even knew what I was doing, my fist was on his cheek.

The fight was a total blur; I just remember seeing red. Angry. I was fucking angry. I still am. But we all have that one thing you don't joke about, right? Like that one thing that's too serious, no way, don't cross that line unless you want to get decked. I'm sure you know what yours is; everyone does. For some people, it's babies dying or suicide or whatever; there are just some things you don't say. And this fucker said it.

Before you start worrying, I'm fine. Few stitches, and they popped my shoulder back into place. I can't even tell you who won. It all felt like a loss to me. The owner told me I was "cut off for a few weeks," essentially completing the holy trinity of lost happy places. My wife. My girlfriend. My bar.

To top things off, the nurse who was checking me out started asking all these questions about my breathing. I tried to explain to her that I'd smoked since I was 14 and that this was pretty normal for me. She nodded, but I could tell she was in her own head. She insisted I come for a few tests. I didn't want to at first, but then I thought, hey, free day off work.

Also, luckily the guy I hit understood I was going through a rough time and didn't press charges. So that's good. I go to the doctor on Monday, I guess I'll keep you posted on that. But seriously, if someone is your happy place, build a fucking house.

                                                Sincerely,
                                                Happy Placeless

December 21

Alright, this is going to be short and sweet. Well, not sweet, actually, bitter.

Long story short, I'm basically dying. No, that's not me being overdramatic in my feelings again. I went back to the doctors; they ran all kinds of tests and asked me all kinds of questions. I tried to explain that I haven't worked out in a while and that I've smoked since I was 14 and that I have spent pretty much my whole life not being able to get a full breath of air.

But I might as well have been talking to a wall. They persisted and refused to let me live comfortably in my innocence. Nope, they had to tell me. They diagnosed me with some obstructive pulmonary something or other, I don't know; I was so angry, the big doctor's words went right over my head.

But they did everything by the book. They gave me a treatment plan that spans over the course of the next year. They warned me that it was a "mildly severe case." How the fuck can you be mildly severe? Like you're diagnosing life-threatening diseases, not naming hot sauces at Taco Bell. I had the nurse from the first time; she stayed the whole time, even put a hand on my shoulder at one point. She seemed to be the kind that really cares. That got into the profession to help people, not to look badass and impress parents. She felt genuine, and in any other point in my life, I would have been thankful for it. But right now, I was just pissed.

So basically, here's the "Plan of attack," as Dr. Just Graduated told me: the first step is pills. Medication to relax the muscles in my lungs or tubes or something like that. Basically, see if my breathing can improve. If in a few months that doesn't work, we will discuss "alternatives."

One of those being, oxygen. Yes, oxygen. You know, like that commercial with the two old ladies, and one is rolling a heavy scuba tank thing. And the one old bitch is in black and white, and a huge red X flashes on the screen; meanwhile, Doretha has the convenient purse thing, and she's in full color, smelling flowers and shit? Yep, I'm a 6'2, 230 pounds 33-year-old man, and Doretha is gonna give me a run for my money.

And finally, the hail-Mary-last-resort-don't-want-to-unless-we-have-to-option is surgery. It's a high-risk one. So that's my option. They also gave me a pamphlet for counseling. The front has this old dude cheesing in his GAP-looking polo with some cliche lady with a blazer and a clipboard. It talked about coping and how to tell loved ones. You know you're screwed when the doc basically hands you cliff notes on how to tell your family you're a goner.

This brought up a whole other worry in my head, telling my family. I mean, I am literally going to my sister's cabin for Christmas tomorrow. Do I tell them? This is already the first year without Penny; I knew it would be rough on all of us. But do I double down on that? Like hey, so yeah, Penny's dead, and I might be next, woo! Ho Ho Ho Merry Christmas!

    I don't think I will. I think I need to get my head on straight before I tell anyone else or let them get involved. Just the smart thing to do; it's just crazy, though. I don't feel any fire. I guess maybe because I'm still in shock, or hell, maybe I'm still numb from these past few months. But I feel no fire, no drive, no fight left in me. Normally when bad things happen, I'm the positive guy, I'm the "we can do this!", pull myself up by my bootstraps kinda guy. But I just don't even care. I don't feel the need to fight at all. And I honestly am not sure what to think of that. But I figured I'm gonna break and tell someone, so I made sure it was you. I don't want to scare anyone yet. Lots of big decisions to make, but right now, I've got to push all of it out of my mind and just focus on the holly jollies and gingerbread.

    But anyway, as I was walking out of the examination room, with my death pamphlets in hand, the doc called out after me, "Hey, looks like that bar fight might have saved your life!" he chuckled. I wanted to punch him. My hand is already very bruised, and it would hurt like a motherfucker, but I wanted to. It didn't save my life; it ended it. Again.... I didn't even know that it was possible to live thru your life-ending, not once but TWICE. Maybe that's why I don't really give a damn if my lungs are able to breathe because my heart stopped beating when Pen's did. First Christmas as a dead man walking. Cool. 'Tis the damn season.

Sincerely,
Doretha 2.0

December 26

Merry Christmas or whatever you celebrate. Hope you had a good holiday. Maybe you got to see family, maybe you just got drunk with your friends and laid under the Christmas tree. I did both. Kinda. My nephew practically tackled me to the ground and pulled me under it with him. It was a nice moment, not sure if it was the eggnog or the blood not rushing to my head or his little hand wrapped around my two middle fingers. But it was peaceful, the kind of moment that even when you are in it, you wish you could pause and live there.

The cabin was beautiful; my sister always went all out to make it look like a Christmas wonderland. It was a strange concept, really, how a bunch of twinkling lights and the smell of gingerbread can make a place we only spent one week a year at feel like home. But it did, and for a split second, under that tree, I felt like I could breathe again. However, my lungs quickly reminded me to stop dreaming.

I tried, though; I really did fucking try. I wore ugly sweaters, I sang the songs, I tried to fill the gaping hole in my chest with icing and gumdrops. I tried to ignore the air between my fingers where she would have been. I tried, I really, really tried.

I tried to ignore it, treat it like the elephant in the room it was. But no one else did; I swear every single person asked me how I was doing. And one thing I learned very quickly is that I can't be honest. Never, ever be honest. It's this unspoken rule that when someone asks you how you're doing, it's for their peace of mind, not yours.

It's just like last year Penny and I was in an aquarium, happily swimming with plenty of rock formations and other people to hide behind. But now, it's like I'm alone in a plastic bag, and everyone keeps shaking it to see if I'm breathing.

The hardest part is the whole week was tainted in Penny. She adored Christmas, well, any holiday, really. She was just a celebratory person, the kind that decorated for like Fourth of July and Valentine's Day and St. Patrick's Day. But Christmas was her season, her time to shine. It was the only time of year she stopped wearing yellow.

She was always prepared with organized checklists of decorations, color-coded totes, and designated work zones. She'd pull the 6 or 7 Christmas totes out the week of Halloween. One year she knew the case she had would take up all her time, so she decorated for Halloween and Christmas at the same time. It was so chaotic and random. Seeing elves and bats together. Orange pumpkins glowing next to glistening fake snowflakes. Santa and Dracula on opposite sides of the coffee maker. It was like living in a Hobby Lobby. But it made her happy, so I couldn't complain. I even surprised her and put up the outside Christmas and Halloween lights, Christmas trees, and skeletons in the middle of October. Yep, our neighbors had to think we were on drugs. But we didn't give a damn. She never cared what anyone thought of her or the things she did. That's one of the reason's I think she was such a good lawyer; she knew her truth and stuck to it no matter what.

Like I said, the entire weekend felt covered in her, like a Penny cloud just loomed over the house. Or maybe it was just on me. Maybe I was walking around in a big fog. But there was one moment, from last year, I couldn't get out of my head.

She had called me to the room to help her find something. She pulled me on the balcony and demanded a cigarette, saying she knew I had some hidden, and she wasn't even mad; she just needed one. I tried to play innocent, claiming I didn't have any.

"Your mother is driving me crazy. So, give me one and cut the shit, Bailer." Was her response. I always knew she was serious when she called me by my last name. Our last name.

Now, this was one of those what I call "grizzly bear situations." Where you can try to do the right thing and argue but then end up feeling the wrath of whatever you're up against. Or you can smile, barricade yourself in the camper and let her destroy the $10 cooler and get what she wants.

So, I showed her my secret stash and let her have one. I remember being in awe of someone looking so cute in a snowman sweater holding a death stick between her fingers.

I asked her what mom was saying even though I'm pretty sure I knew the answer: babies.

"It's not that I don't want kids; it's just I don't know if I'm ready for it. I mean, yes, with the promotion, I would have more flexibility. And I know your parents would help out, and maybe we..." she rambled on and on.

I explained to her that no one is ever truly ready. And that no matter when we decide it's time, we are just going to have to figure it out as we go.

"So, we just wing it and pray they don't become serial killers?" she laughed, but I could see the true worry in her eyes. I got her calmed down and told her not to let my mom or anyone psych her out. "We have all the time in the world."

Yep, I really said that, fucking idiot. We stood out there for a long minute, huddled in a blanket. Eventually, she said we could start trying. Well, actually, her words were "stop not trying," but the same thing.

"Whatever happens, happens." Was the agreement we made over our last cigarettes ever. Watching cute little red birds peck at the snow, soaking up the wintery landscape. Living what I had no idea was the best years of my life.

Now, I stand here, a year later. Same balcony, different cigarette. There's no snow, no birds; everything was just cold, brown, and dead.

Well, that's a damn near the perfect transition to why I'm actually writing to you. I've done some research on this condition, the treatments are only defensive, not redhibitory. Basically, it's like putting a swimming pool in the middle of a burned house. It won't fix the damage, but it will help prevent another fire. But the walls can still crumble, the floor can still cave in. It's basically all guesswork.

And even if everything goes exactly as planned, they say I MIGHT have two years. That's it. Two years. 520 days. Two bittersweet birthdays. Two more years of work and traffic and silent elevator rides. Two more fishbowl Christmases. Honestly, I don't think it's worth it for me.

So, I'm gonna shoot ya straight. By well... shooting me straight. Ha. Wow. Okay, maybe that was a little dark. But seriously, I think it would be better to go out on my own terms.

So, on January 1, I will be taking my own life. It just seems perfect. It's a new year, it's my birthday, so I have an even number on my time clock. Let the world start a new year without me. But in order to provide a little bit of closure, I will be writing one goodbye letter every day. I don't want you or anyone else thinking I just snapped. That this was just a drunken mistake or a momentary lapse in judgment. I don't expect you to understand, but thanks for listening anyway.

Sincerely,
Soon at Peace

December 27

Mom, do you remember when Grandpa died? I was like 6 and had no grasp on the concept of death. You spent the night curled up in my twin-sized bed, telling me of this magical land: heaven. You painted these beautiful mental pictures of golden roads and cotton candy clouds. You told me of warm glowing lights that are always lit and rainbows that were touchable; you could play with them like Play-Doh. You told me they have a postal system and can send us messages whenever we need them to. You told me of signs and signals you'd seen throughout your life. You promised me that the bridge between our world and that one was "as unbreakable as God himself." And if I wanted to see Grampy, all I had to do was ask.

I tested your theory many times over the years; he always showed up. Sometimes in a rainbow, sometimes a song, sometimes just a strong breeze. But one, I could feel him in.

Admittedly, I strayed from God. You know, I became a punk-ass teenager. Then a self-centered college kid who didn't give Him a second thought. Then a working adult who was just too busy. And now I guess I'm so mad at him; we aren't on speaking terms.

I lost faith. I quit going to church. All the verses I have had pounded into my head fell out. But one thing I never lost faith in was the concept of heaven. Even when I saw men die in unspeakable ways, I found myself praying for them and silently telling them to enjoy the cotton candy clouds and to send a breeze when they make it okay.

I like to believe it's true. And I like to believe our God is a forgiving one. That all those songs you made me get up and sing with the smelly kids about Him always loving his children are true. Maybe, he'll let me in on a technicality. Maybe Penny gets a plus-one. I don't know, but I do know that I am going into this with faith because of you. And only because of you.

This isn't easy for me to say. I don't know what to say, actually; what do you say to the most important person in your life when you know it's going to hurt them?

So, here's what I've decided: this letter is for closure, not comfort.

When I was in 8th grade, and those jerks used to pick on me, you told me to own it, to steer into the skid, take back the narrative, and do what I felt like was best for me. Well, this is me doing that.

I hate this. I hate that this is going to break you. I hate that this is bringing you the one thing you've spent 33 years praying against. I'm so sorry it's this way. I feel like there could have been easier ways for this. Maybe falling out of the treehouse you always hated? Or in the desert? Maybe two soldiers waiting for your porch light would have been easier.

Instead of a letter, but a wise woman once told me, ""You can't change the hand you were dealt, only how you play it." Well, this is me playing it. I don't want to live like this. Stuck. Trapped. Locked into situations, I can't beat. All without the one person who is supposed to be by my side.

    Penny was my everything. She kept me going, she held me when the world went dark. They say you end up with someone like your parents, and she was a hell of a lot like you. She was the tough one, she held the umbrella when the sky started falling, she saved me, mama, in a way no one ever could.

    As much as I love you, as strong as you made me, I can't do this without her. And this disease is a way out. It's not a matter of if, but when.

    But I want, no, I NEED you to know that I am at peace, I'm steering into the skid. My terms. My timing. I'm okay, I'm not drunk or high. It's better this way, trust me.

    I want to thank you for every single beautiful, heartbreaking, hilarious, incredible, astonishing, breathtaking, amazing second of this life you have given me. I would be nothing without you, but please don't be nothing without me. Don't you fucking (sorry language) dare let this kill you too. You keep living. Swim in the ocean. Keep filming firework shows even though you never watch the videos again. Eat all the tacos you can, and go for hikes every now and again. And if heaven turns out to be real, look for me. I'll try to rustle some leaves for ya. I love you, mama more than words could ever explain.

                                          Sincerely,
                                        Your Schmoogerbooger

December 28

Dad,

Hey, so again, not really sure what to say, I guess I should get the technical stuff out of the way before I get to any gooey shit.

My will is in the safe in the closet. My social and birth certificate are in there as well. My bank account password is "scottyblue12", same with the login for my ROTH. Take that money and do some good with it. Donate some of it. Take Mom swimming with the ponies in Aruba. Put some aside for Lindsey and Jacob, college fund or wedding fund or if they open their own business, a graduation gift from ole' Uncle Airplane.

Alright, mushy stuff, I know you well enough to know exactly how you are going to handle this. You are going to shut down, you'll be there for mom and Sarah and Michael, but you won't be there for yourself. You'll push everything you're feeling down until you explode. And the damage won't be pretty. Trust me.

Now there are a few things I need to get off my chest. Firstly, Bobby Callen didn't break the house window; I did. I threw the baseball. I was 7 and terrified, so I lied. When I was 15 at the beach house, and you caught me "sleepwalking," I was drunk. Yeah, Sarah snuck me out. I had no concept of pacing, and I was hammered, so she covered for me. I once took $100 out of your wallet to buy weed. Oh shit, yeah, I smoked in college. I don't anymore. Freshman year, I never tried out for football. I know it was your dream, but I sucked, and I hated it. So, I told you I didn't make the team.

I wrote you four or five letters while on deployment, but I always chickened out sending them. So, I just added "and Dad" to mom's letters. And the last thing is a big one. And this is quite literally the only circumstance I would ever tell you, Natalya. You were so mad at me for letting her "get away", I felt like I was letting you down, but the truth is she abused me. We got back together a few months ago, and both times, I broke up with her. She hurt me, physically, verbally and emotionally. She assaulted me. I didn't fall off the counter into a wine rack. She broke the glasses on me. She left bruises and even hospitalized me. She manipulated and tore me down to the point I didn't know who I was. She was my abuser, and it took me a long fucking time to admit that.

I mean, I'm a man. A goddamn solider. How can I say a little woman with ruby pink nail polish is my abuser? I felt like I should be ashamed or that I was over exaggerating.

But I'm not. She hurt me. She tracked me. She controlled me and told me I was worthless without her, so many times I believed it. And I thought that made me weak, but I realized she only had this control because I loved her. I was strong enough to trust her and let my guard down. And I got fucking burned for it, but I still did it. It took a lot of strength to open up to her, and twice that amount to admit it to myself. But now that I have, I can admit it to you. And maybe earn a drop of your respect back.

I don't want you to think I'm giving up, I'm not. This is just getting there faster. I don't want to fall apart. I don't want to break and be hooked up to a bunch of beeping machines doing what my body is supposed to. I don't want to turn all grey and skinny, shell of a man.

And more importantly, I don't want you all to remember me that way. I want y'all to remember me as me: big goober with huge teeth. Laughing at stupid puns and fart jokes. Always wearing that 25-year-old Cayotes hat, his pops got him at his first game. Remember me scaring people with that falling apart Jason mask. Remember my charcoal burgers. My "glowstick dance." All of it.

I hope you can understand this someday. Not now; I get that. But someday. But in the meantime, there are a few things you need to promise me. Promise me. Your dying son.

1. You take care of the family that includes yourself.
2. You feel this. Don't bottle it up. Don't ignore it. Don't die with me. Don't sit at home watching the news hating the world. It's not as bad as you think.
3. Download Snapchat. Make up some fake name and add Michael. Snapchat is where all the youngins hide everything, so you'll need to keep an eye on him. Don't use my account that would freak him out.

4. Don't drink. Mr. Daniels is a great pal to celebrate with, but don't let him move in.
5. Remember me as I lived, not as I died.
6. Forgive me.

    I know that's a tough list, but you are the greatest man I've ever known. I know you can do this. I may have hated living in the shadow of your greatness as a kid, but I realize now, it was an honor. Thank you for everything.

                  Love,
                    Your "Sport" that sucked at sports

December 29

Sarah,

Hey sis, so this isn't easy. And I'm sure by now you've figured out why. And I'm sure you aren't happy about it. And knowing my luck, I'm probably stealing the spotlight from you. Again. Feels like I always do. Me winning that grant the day you graduated. Getting deployed when you got engaged. Bringing Penny home when you announced you were pregnant. I always stole your thunder, and I'm sorry. I don't mean to, I swear.

I've always looked up to you. You were always so much better of a person than me. But it seems like I always got the easy breaks. I guess you could say it caught up to me; looks like with me dying first, the world finally got one right.

I know this is going to hurt you, I know you are going to find a way to blame yourself. Don't. You couldn't have saved me. Christmas was lovely; thank you for hosting every year; you nail it every time.

You were an awesome sister, and you always made me feel included even when I'm sure there were times you didn't want me there.

There are a few things I would like to apologize for: I'm sorry; I hid your gym bag and got you in trouble. I'm sorry I broke your piggy bank. I'm sorry I was a 15-year-old idiot who did 6 tequila shots, and threw up in your car. I'm sorry I walked in on you and Harley and didn't take the hint to leave, you guys were trying to fuck; I realize that now. But I mean, his name was Harley, and he had a wallet on a chain, I might have done you a favor. I'm sorry we've been distant the past few years, it wasn't either of our faults just got busy, we weren't those kids performing full-on setlists washing your car.

I am so proud of you. You have created yourself a beautiful life. You're a great sister, an amazing mom to Lindsey and Jacob, and clearly the golden child of the family. I'm very thankful to have had the chance to share my life with you. From all the bedsheet rocket ships to my wedding day, you took every step with me.

And I know you would want to be here now, you'd be going crazy researching treatments, probably dragging me to some "healer" that would sage me, rub crystals on my balls and charge you $300 for it. Ha, you would over fluff my pillows and bring me ABC soup with swear words spelled out in it.

You'd try to fix me, you'd try to save me, and that's why for once, I'm thankful for the 2094 miles between us because you can't. You can't save me, and this way, you can't try and fail to. You just have to accept it. You have to let me go. And you know if there is a way, I'll be there. I'll try to watch over Lindsey and Jacob, please tell them their uncle Airplane loves them very, very, very much.

I'm gonna miss throwing those little buggers around. Lean on Todd. Don't push him away. And tell him fuck the Bruins while you're at it. Tell him despite all the hockey rivalry and the shit talk; he's actually really good for you,

And I'm proud of him for that. I'm proud of you. You were always the best role model for me. I never tell you nearly enough, but I love you. You did good. You did really, really good.

       Love,
       The biggest pain in your ass ever

December 30

Little Dude,

    Hey bro, so you get a different type of letter, I've spent days thinking of all the things I want to tell you, and dude, there is too much to put in one letter. I mean, you're a fucking kid, I am supposed to pack a lifetime of advice into one letter? Crazy, Nah, Not doing it.
    So in my closet, there is a box of 10 letters:

1. For your first day of college (yes, you are going end of the discussion, and you can't argue with a dead guy).
2. When you lose your virginity (relax, it's not graphic).
3. When you are about to propose (yeah, you say you don't want to get married, but we all say that)
4. When you find a job that makes you happy
5. Your wedding day
6. Your first fight with your wife.
7. When mom dies.
8. When dad dies.
9. The day you become a dad and the 10th one is for the worst day of your life, whenever that may be, tomorrow or 30 years from now,

    Save it, don't rush into it. And yes, I'm totally hypocritical and go on a long rant about how life is precious and always worth living. But you need to understand our circumstances are different. I realize that I'm not going to be there for all those moments, so this is the best I can do. I'm also going to give you a bunch of random advice that I was planning on sprinkling in over the years, but here we go:

- Don't bring your card to a casino. Bring cash, and when you are done, you're done.
- Redheads are as psycho as the rumors. It's fun, but if knives or "potions" come out, RUN.
- Tell people you love them. Even your boys. It's not gay to care.
- Get into a fight. It'll change you. But don't throw the first punch; that's a dick move.
- Don't ruin your career over a girl. No matter how hot.
- Buy suits. Rent tuxedos.
- If you can act like an idiot, talk about your dreams and cry in front of her, She's the one.
- Don't drink when you are sad, only when you are having fun.
- Don't chug a warm beer.
- Puking in an uber is a $200 fine
- Don't forget about God; He will be there when no one else is.
- Cheer for your team even when they are losing. Loyalty outweighs victory.
- Make an effort to remember the little things. The outfit she wears on the first date. The song mom sings around the house. Sarah's favorite flower. Your best friend's favorite book. Little

things about the people you love. It will mean more than you realize.
- You don't get do-overs.
- True friends only lie when they are hiding a surprise party. No other time.
- Being tough doesn't mean being emotionless
- Any movie series that has more than three sucks; save your money (Exception: Marvel)
- Don't apologize for any part of you.
- Don't work your life away; life is more than cashing paychecks.
- You'll regret not doing things more than you'll regret doing them.
- Don't forget your family, whether it's college or a job, or a wife, don't forget your family. Never be too busy for the ones that love you.

If you ever don't know what to do, just pause, look up at the clouds and think, what would my big brother do? Then do the exact opposite... Ha, seriously, though, you'll be good. You'll do great things, I know it. Why? Because you're my little dude. And you'll always be my little dude. Love you turdmunch.

Sincerely,
Big Dude

December 30

Alright, blurbs to everyone else.

1. Nick,

Well, boss, I guess this is my two weeks. You were so annoying. You need to learn respect from other people, especially the people you needed to get you where you want to go. You are over-confident, and you don't have the brains to back your balls. You're a kid that needs a reality check. Maybe a dead guy calling you a piece of shit will be enough. Fix yourself, bro.

2. Bryan,

You have become a great friend to me. And I am blessed to have called you all, bros. You were my bartender, a fight referee, an unpaid therapist, and a hell of a man. I'm going to leave my cards with Annalise. buy everyone a round or two on me. Take care of them all. Swipe it till it declines, and toast to me when you feel like it. Don't pour it out for me. That's just a waste.

December 31

Lise,

    I'm not going to lie; I've been putting this one-off big time. This is one of the hardest ones I've had to do. So hard, in fact, I almost didn't do it. But I knew if I left you without a goodbye, you would come to the afterlife just to kick my ass. I don't know what to say, but I'm gonna try.

    Do you remember when we met? I was a young dumb hotshot who thought I could pull anyone I wanted. And you couldn't care less if I existed. And when I tried introducing myself, you glared into my soul and said, "Okay and...?"

    God, you knocked me right off my pedestal. I had never met someone who wasn't falling to my feet.

    Eventually, you told me your name was Annalise, but everyone calls you Anna. My smartass mouth asked why you preferred the first half of your name.

    You rolled your eyes and said, "Because Anna is a name. Lease is what you sign for a car." And I said I was going to call you "Lise" from now on, and you scoffed and said, "right, like I am ever going to see you again." And I insisted you would.

    Well, I am not one to gloat, but it's been 10 years of friendship, darlin'. I was right. And I don't think I have ever called you by your full name.

You're my best friend, dude. You've been there for me in every way I could have imagined. You've walked by my side through hells that had nothing to do with you: the foot surgery, the Natalya fiasco... both of them... You were there the day I signed my life away, and the day I got it back.

You helped me with Penny, smacked some sense into me, and helped me propose. You even wore those 10-year-old star shoes that were 2 sizes too small for our wedding because Penny heard you say they were good luck. You always did everything you could for her. And me, I always tried to be there for you, and you may think that this letter is the end of that agreement. Wrong kiddo.

If there is an afterlife, I will be on you like white on rice. Well, white on white rice, there isn't white on yellow rice or brown rice, but you get what I'm saying. I would like to inform you that Penny and I will personally be haunting any guy that isn't good enough for you. Like, oh, you got a new man? Is he hiding texts? Well, I hope he likes starved demons shoved up his asshole! I told everyone else to look for me in the breeze or on the radio, but you? Nah. You'll see me when your cheating boyfriend's dick randomly turns green. It gives a whole new meaning to the term "ghosting."

See, I hope that that totally true statement made you laugh. I know you are going to be crying. You are going to be mad. Furious even. And that's okay. I don't expect you to understand. But I hope one day you can forgive me.

I need you to understand there is nothing you could have done. I don't want you spending your life wondering if you had just hugged me one more time or brought me one more chicken pot pie, it would have made a difference. It wouldn't have. My lungs are failing. I am going to die. I can't change that. But I can take control and do what I have to do.

And if we are being honest, I thought about having you with me. I thought about overdosing on sleeping pills instead. Having you hold my hand, listen to you tell the story of the time you wrecked your car over a bird. You'd pull your hair up in the scrunchie you got when all of us went to Tennessee. Because I know your hair falls in your face when you cry. You'd wear the Two Door Saloon shirt that our friendship was built on. I'd wear my Cayotes shirt (as if I would even consider dying in anything else).

I'd go out of this life the same way I lived it: laughing with my best friend. If I can't die holding Penny's hand, I'd want to die holding yours. But I realized you'd never let me go. Watching me die would be far worse than you seeing me dead. You would try to stop me. Your mind wouldn't comprehend, and it would scar you. I have dealt with those kinds of scars my whole life. I can't do that to you. As much as it would comfort me, it would destroy you. That isn't fair to you; you didn't ask for this. You didn't choose it; I can't choose it for you. I thought about it deeply but ultimately decided this is something I need to do on my own. That and pill suicide have higher failure rates. A bullet is just easier.

Another thing I want you to know is you are going to find it. You are going to find the kind of love Penny and I had. I know you are always so worried about it but don't be, he is going to respect you without trying to diminish your glow. He's going to love you but not baby you. He's going to know your favorite ice cream is strawberry (gross.). He's going to know to put silverware in the dishwasher "pointy side down." He's going to come home with matching sweaters for Slink and Lucy. Oh yeah... can you take Lucy? For me? Please, your dead best friend. And I promise I won't ever use the dying card again. I just don't want her to end up alone in a shelter. Plus, she and Slink are already besties. I'll pack up her stuff for you; I appreciate it greatly. Anyway, back on track, you are going to find that love; you deserve it. So, don't you fucking dare settle for less.

Don't you dare fucking shrink yourself to not intimidate someone. Real men will respect you for your boldness, not run from it. Don't let these little bitch boys get you down.

God, there is so much I want to tell you. Or maybe I am just pushing it so time will go by faster. It's getting later, we are getting closer. I am actually excited. I'm excited to be free. I am very sorry for the pain it will cause you and my family. If I could take it with me, I would. But this is just something I need to do. So, I will leave you with this:

1. You will be okay.
2. You will find an amazing, great, true love. Don't settle.
3. Remember, don't put champagne in the freezer.
4. Hit the bird, not the tree.

5. I will always love you, kid.

Seriously, you don't understand how hard it is to write this. I can't imagine how hard it will be to read. But I just need you to understand this is something I have to do. This is the right thing for me to do. I hope you can forgive me. Hope you still love me.

                    Sincerely,
                    Forever the Polka Dot Cowboy

January 1

Surprise. It's me. So funny story. You ever fuck up or almost fuck up so bad that God steps in and essentially bitch-slaps you? Well, that's basically what happened.

I was done. Honestly, I was ready. Thought of every detail. Packed up my whole house, so my family didn't have to. Had my notarized will on the kitchen table. I tossed out all perishable food and bagged the rest to be donated. I hung plastic shower curtains on the wall and covered the entire floor. I did some research, and the range I'll be firing at shouldn't cause a huge splatter but just in case. I wasn't quite sure what to do with my old uniforms, but to be fair, I never knew what to do with them when I got out in the first place. So, I took the nameplates off, put the rest in the bag to be donated. Maybe some new recruit will get them, or maybe some teenage brat will use them in a play. I didn't really care. All the paperwork at work had been done for the next week. My co-worker asked me if I was going on vacation. Ha. Kinda.

I was ready. I cleaned my gun to ensure it wouldn't jam. I decided to go through my chest, quicker death, less chance of survival. Plus, my mama would want to see my face in the casket. I can't take that from her. Besides, I liked the poetic nature of end it all where it began.

So, I got off work, practically giddy, I stopped at the ice cream shop on 4th, tipped the guy $100; I mean hell, I wasn't going to need it. I took a shower, I thought of shaving my beard, just for the hell of it. But I'd spent years growing it; it felt like a going down with the ship kind of thing.

I thought about putting on my Cayotes shirt, as I had told Annalise in her goodbye, I wouldn't want to die in anything else. But then I realized she might want it. It might be a comfort to her, and I was making it where she loses two of her best friends in less than four months. I owed her every comfort I could give her. So, I folded it neatly on the table.

I resumed getting dressed. Nice slacks, red button-down. Even though it probably won't make too much of a difference, I figure it might conceal some of the bloodstains. Slightly less traumatic for my neighbor when he finds me. I also put on a diaper. Itchy son-of-a-bitch, but bodies defecate after death. Another thing that I didn't want my neighbor to have to deal with.

I had to laugh while I was putting it on; I remembered the poor cashier's face. She was a cute, teenage-looking blonde. She tried to hide her confusion when a huge, tatted, bearded 33-year-old dude was buying cigarettes, adult diapers, bubble wrap, and a Red Bull.

Anyway, I finished getting dressed and looked in the mirror. I looked good. Like GQ model level good. Everything but my eyes. They were tired.

At the last minute, I decided to take my shoes off. Michael had given them to me, and perhaps he'd like to grow into them. Wear them on big job interviews or his wedding day. a way to feel his big bro with him. He'd use them to honor me.

This actually brought up an interesting conversation in my head. How people would take it? How would they mourn? How would they honor me?

Lise would get a tattoo; I'm almost sure of it. Who would come to my funeral? Who would cry? Who would play it strong but punch a hole in the wall when they got home? It got to me, thinking of all the inside jokes I wouldn't get to be a part of. All the funerals and weddings I'd never get to pay my respects to. The children born, I'd never know. For a split second, this was almost enough to change my mind. But I coughed and was painfully reminded why I was doing this.

Control. I wasn't going to hear those jokes or baby giggles anyway.

My phone alarm went off. 11:59. This is it. I turned and looked at the shower curtain that would soon be a canvas of my escape. A masterpiece I'd never get to see. I had the TV on; I figured the countdown might help. Millions of people chanting 20...19...18 kinds of puts the pressure on. No way to chicken out. But damn, those last 10 seconds felt like eternities.

10. I took the deepest breath I could
9. I turned the safety off
8. I looked around
7. I wiggled my toes; they stuck to the plastic
6. I put the gun to my chest

5. I send a mental "I love you" to everyone I can think of

4. I ask for mercy on my soul

3. I close my eyes

2. I see Penny

Milliseconds before they reached one, milliseconds before my finger squeezed. Lucy started screaming and not howling or barking, screaming like a child. In a way, I had never heard before. My heart takes over, and I put the gun down and run to find her.

I walk into the bedroom and see her fluffy hind legs sticking out from underneath the bed. Her fat ass had gotten stuck. I pulled her out, silently cursing her for ruining my perfect ending. She got out, looked me dead in the eyes darted right back under, this time flipping on her back. I pulled and pulled, but she would not come out. Eventually, I crawled under there to see what she was so obsessed with. She pushed her nose up to the rungs of the bed frame. Specifically, to a piece of folded paper. I grabbed it, and she immediately pulled out. After sliding myself out and adjusting, I opened the paper.

It was Penny's bucket list. I had never seen it before. I can't explain to you the pleasure of seeing something of hers "new." She had made a list of 20 things she wanted to do before she died. And my heart shattered onto the carpet when I realized only half the boxes were checked.

That's when God bitch-slapped me. I can't be done here because she's not done here. If she couldn't do everything on this list, then I have to finish it for her. That way, if there's a chance I'll pass her in the afterlife, I can at least say we did it.

So, don't get all emotional on me. Fuck being happy. Fuck fighting to live. This wasn't an "I'm saved" moment; this was a "not yet" moment.

So that's the reason, and the ONLY reason I put the gun away for now. Simply: she's not done, so I'm not done. It's that easy. So, needless to say, looks like you're stuck talking to me for a little while longer. Sorry.

Sincerely,
Accidentally 34

January 6

I realize you might be wondering how I'm doing since I didn't get a bite of the steel sausage. I honestly feel no different, I guess nothing really changed. Like I said, it was a "not yet moment."

The best way I can describe it is, have you ever gotten invited to a party? And you were so excited, so happy, you started getting ready like 3 hours early. Showering, shaving, ironing your best clothes. You get fully ready to go, and then you get a text saying it's been rescheduled. So, you just sit there, on the edge of your bed, fully dressed, unsure of what to do with yourself.

That's me right now. Things are stagnant, hazy my whole life feels like that in-between of sleep, where your body is paralyzed, but your mind is active. That's how it feels; I'm all prettied up with nowhere to go.

And worse off, I don't know what to say, who to tell, who not to tell. I already know how they would all react. Annalise would go into overdrive and smother me. Crying, probably hit my arm a time or two. She would try her damnedest to save me. She'd throw away all my knives and sell all my guns. She would let protecting me consume her until she was nothing else. And in the end, I would still let her down.

My boys wouldn't know how to react. They are good men but don't handle the serious stuff well. I'd probably end up getting made fun of and feeling even shittier. And then they would feel guilty at my funeral. Probably turn to unhealthy options of coping like alcohol or adultery. I can't ruin their lives just because mine is over.

My parents would see me as their child. Their parenting glasses would fall onto their noses, and I would suddenly morph into a six-year-old in rocket ship footed pajamas, hugging my stuffed lion in one hand and a "big boy cup" full of chock-y milk in the other. They would go into Mama bear mode and probably do something crazy like move here. That would be too much. Plus, then there is a chance they would be the ones to find my body. And that's not fair to them either.

So, I guess that leaves you... which is why I told you what happened. At least that's the only reason I could think of, just so I can get it out. Open up to you so I can be locked up tight to the rest of the world. That's the only thing I can think of as to why I'm still writing. I mean, this isn't a memoir. It's not going to be hung in the Smithsonian someday. Nah. No one cares about me or my story. So, I can say whatever the hell I want to.

I think that's what you are for me: freedom. I don't have to keep up the charade of being okay. I don't have to hold down my coughing fits or leave when they get too bad. I can say it freely: I am dying. I mean, we all are dying technically, but I'm dying faster than most. Ha. I say that like it's bragging rights. Anyway, I'm dying. I wish I was dead already, but God or the universe or whatever said I wasn't done yet, so I guess that means I'm still here for a bit.

That's one thing I love about you, I don't have to bullshit. No lies. No secrets. Just truth. And since we are being honest, I have no idea what to do now.

           Sincerely,
           Still Got My Party Shoes On

January 14

Why do women always feel the need to meddle? Get all wrapped up in other people's emotions. Lise signed us up for this stupid grief class. Her grandpa, who practically raised her, died last year, and she thinks me dating Nat was a "cry for help." So, she forced me to go with her and sit in the sad circle and explain what happened. The first assignment was to write my life story to read to the class next week.

I am supposed to start a new journal, but no, I am a grown man; having one is embarrassing enough, let alone two. So, here's what we are going to do we are going to pretend this is brand new, and I'll read this to the stupid group. Okay? Okay. Life story in 3...2...1...

I was born on January 1; I'm 34. I was raised in the suburbs of a decent-sized city. So, I had the best of worlds. Had a normal childhood. Parents were awesome. I grew up with a few really good friends instead of a lot of fake ones.

I've had a few girlfriends throughout high school. I was in the band. Played trumpet. At 17, I got a job bussing at a bar; I met a waitress named Annalise, who is now my best friend and the one who dragged me here today.

Anyway, I joined the military at 18. Did that for 8 years, got out, went to college for business. While in school, I got a job bartending. When I was 26, I met the love of my life: Penny. We got married after 3 years of dating. We were together 7 years in total. And she was murdered 5 months ago. And that brings me to here.

*DON'T READ OUT LOUD. Okay, I know, I know that would have been the perfect time to tell Annalise I'm dying and about my little death party. But I can't. Not in front of strangers. When and if I was going to tell her any of this, it has to be when we were alone. When I could hold her, where she could hit me and cry and scream profanity as much as she wanted to. I'll tell her. Eventually. I mean, how else am I going to explain me randomly going on trips all of a sudden.

I am not prepared for that conversation at all. I never know what to say. Like ever. Even with this stupid summary thing. The guy said only the important things. How do I determine what is important? Like if I said, okay, make me a chronological bullet-point timeline of your life, what would you put? The moments that you remember most or the moments the world cares about? The ones where you remember every detail down to the pattern on your socks or the big glossed-over moments? It's actually quite a challenging task. Or maybe I just overthink everything literally.

Sincerely,
Man, With ONE Journal

January 16

I need your help. As crazy as that sounds, I think I am going to tell my family my plan. At least the finishing Penny's list and the shitty failing lungs part. I know that they are not going to understand my decision to refuse treatment. I've mentioned that, right? That I'm just going to finish the list and then go through with my original plan.

I feel awful keeping this secret from them. How close are you with your family? Because I feel like mine is unusually close. We have always been that annoyingly tight open arms no matter what family. The kind that talks about everything and anything.

Especially me and my mom. Like whenever someone asks what relationship I have with my mom, I say she is my best friend. Which depending on how you and your mother is, it makes me look either really sweet or really creepy.

Regardless, she deserves to know. They deserve a chance to process it. I know that if it was reversed, I would want a warning. Plus, this way, they can yell and take their anger out on me instead of each other. It just feels like the right thing to do.

But what the hell do I say? I suck with words (as I'm sure you can validate). Like when you have to call someone, do you practice what you have to say? Well, I do; I go over the imaginary script a million times before

I dial a single number. But how do I prepare for THIS conversation? It took me three days to call the cable company to cancel my subscription. How am I supposed to call the people I love most in the world that God is canceling my life subscription? How the hell am I supposed to do this?

Sincerely,
I'm Actually Asking

January 17

I did it. I told everyone, except Annalise. I am not ready for that one yet. But I called Mom and Dad. And, of course, they didn't understand. They were all like, "Screw the odds!" and "You can fight this!". They don't seem to understand I don't have any fight left in me.

They have always had such faith in me, SO MUCH. Like honestly, that's the only thing I'd change about the way I was raised. They told me I was incredible and extraordinary. Then you get out into the real world, and everyone is extraordinary. But that's the only thing I would change. Which makes me sound like a horrible person, but I think we all have at least one thing we'd change if we could, right?

But if I ever have kids... Well, clearly, I'm not going to, but if I ever did, I would want them to have a good balance between dreams and reality. Like yes, you are amazing, but you're gonna have to work your ass off to prove that to the rest of the world. You don't become legendary by accident. Damn. That's some motivational poster shit right there. Feel free to use that one, first one is free.

Anyway, back on track, phone calls. Mom and Dad freaked, Sarah cried, Michael oddly enough understood. A little too well, it worried me. Actually, It wasn't an easy decision to make. I was hugely debating on telling them at all. But oddly enough, Annalise unknowingly made the decision for me.

    We were at a pizza place eating, just catching up. Then in the middle of the meal, she hopped up and started talking to the random girl waiting at the table a few away from us. They talked for a moment then hugged and then she came back. She explained that that girl had lipstick on her teeth, and she wanted to let her know. I asked her why she did that, why she put herself in an awkward situation just to help some random stranger.

    "Oh, come on, what if it was you with lipstick on your teeth?" she laughed.

    I laughed at first, too. But then what she said next made one of the hardest choices of my life easy.

    "If you were headed towards something that was going to upset you, wouldn't you want a heads-up?"

    That hit me like a ton of bricks. That old tile scratchy ceiling that every place in America has might as well have caved in on me. What if it was reversed? What if my mom was sick? Or my dad? Would I want to know? Would I want the chance to say goodbye? Or would I prefer a blindside? Nope, I would want to know. So I called. And it was awful. Painful. Brutal. Horrible. And now I feel even worse. Yay.

                                  Sincerely,
                              Lipstick Life Lessons

February 2

Not going to lie; I'm a little drunk, I'm not even sure why I keep coming back to this. To you. But here we are. It's her birthday. I don't know if it should say it "is her birthday" or "was her birthday" because it still is the day even if she isn't here. I don't know, I fucking suck at this whole past tense thing.

I suck at a lot of things these days. I haven't gotten out of bed; I finished a bottle of whiskey, and I'd love to grab the other one in the kitchen, but I can't. I can't move. These cotton sheets have turned to cement. I've only gotten up once to answer the aggressive doorbell.

Wish I hadn't. It was a delivery guy bringing a bouquet? Bou... Jesus Christ, FLOWERS, God damn. Stupid French words. I forgot I had ordered them months ago. It was a mix of sunflowers and red roses.

She loved roses and adored sunflowers. Anything yellow actually. She fucking loves yellow. I never cared for it before her. But a few months into our relationship, it had become my favorite too. I would have painted every wall, floor, and ceiling with it if she'd let me. I told her that one time and she laughed. Said I was "missing the point of it." Not really sure how a color can have a point, but she said that it was her favorite part.

"Yellow is only wonderful when there is darkness to make it pop. Too much yellow is just a headache." She said. God, I remember every detail of that moment.

Her hair braided in two pigtails. Ripped up handmade jean shorts, black crop top with (you guessed it) a sunflower on it. She was so happy, so smart, so full of both wonderment and wisdom.

Her theory made sense, but now, the yellow "sprinkled in" doesn't feel as magical as it used to. It didn't give me the "your insides are covered in stardust" feeling she always described. Now yellow feels empty. It feels like a hole. A bunch of tiny holes. Like I'm living in a piece of cheese.

I don't know what to do with the flowers. I know where they should go, but I'm not ready for that shit. Not yet. To see the newness fading in the dirt. To see the stone with the absolute last name I ever wanted to be carved, slowly weathering. I can't. Maybe I will drop them off at the old lady across the street's house. Give the old bird a smile.

Anyway, I know I am in no state of mind to be making life choices. But this solidifies my death choice. I can't do this year after year. Birthdays without excited squeals or post-party hallway sex, Christmas without her now this, it's just not right. I'm not supposed to live this way, so I'm just going to not live.

I don't know, I'm a mess. I can barely see straight. I feel numb, and I hate it. I am so mad at being numb; you think that would make me feel angry and not numb. But no, it's both. Separately, but at the same time. If that makes any damn sense.

But I just wish it was flipped. She should be here. She should be swirling in a numb anger cocktail and crying over the flowers her dead husband sent her. Or hell, if she had to go, Take both of us. That would have been right. I mean, the woman spent her entire adult life fighting for justice; the least God could do give her that. Two lives, one bullet. That's the way it should have been if she had to die for some stupid-ridiculous-bigger-picture-god-only-fucking-knows reason. Then it should have been both of us.

      Sincerely,
      Missed the BOGO Coffin Sale

February 11

Today's assignment in grief club was to write about something normal that annoys us. Something that just irks the living hell out of you that everyone else seems fine with. Well, after sorting through many, many topics, this one just seemed fitting. So here we go.

Today's topic: Valentine's Day.

It's bullshit. Like seriously, who besides jewelers, chocolate companies, and flower shops who actually benefit from this ridiculous affair? Ok, before you go defending "romance," hear me out.

It's not romantic. It doesn't provide couples with security or support. All it does is put pressure on both individuals. Kind gestures become valueless due to the over anticipated expression of them. (How's that for some big boy words?) Flowers sent to your office on a random Monday in May say, "I love you." Flowers sent to your office on Valentine's Day say, "I don't want anyone to doubt that I love you." It's a mandatory expression of love. MANDATORY. It's involuntary and, most of the time, thoughtless. It doesn't show love; it shows you can give in to societal pressure.

And for the singles, it's even worse. It's a day where they use their status to judge their worth. A day that makes falling in love a check box on a To-Do list. Sure, they laugh and scoff with their friends, saying it's just a stupid corporate holiday. But then stay up till 2 a.m. taking personality tests and checking horoscopes, trying to pinpoint the key flaw that has deemed them unlovable. Or even worse than that, they drown their standards in a bottle and swipe their way into a desperate act of conformity. And they don't end up loved. They end up used. They sit up, convincing themselves that a quick-fix-cookie-cutter love is better than waiting for something incredible. Bottom line. It's stupid. For every chocolate heart box opened, there is a human heart broken.

Then don't even get me started on us in the W-club. Widows, and widowers. Man, that's just a day full of reminders of what we watched go into the ground. The flowers are just like the ones we put on her casket. The chocolate is the same taste as the cake at the wake. The commercials and the billboards all flashing reminders of what we no longer have.

It's just awful for everyone. People in love get a momentary, fake sense of stability. Single people end up sad and alone or with someone and even lonelier. And us widow peeps are stuck in a giant neon snow globe of what we lost and want to fling ourselves off a bridge to get away from it. No one wins, and everyone loses something.

Sincerely,
Let's Shoot Cupid with a
Different Kind of Arrow

February 14

Yep, stupid Valentine's Day. And of course, my company is trying to boost morale, so they had a mandatory party because nothing says good times better than required fun.

So, I went and stood in a stupid room, covered in stupid pink and red hearts and glitter. I listened to stories I didn't give a fuck about. I laughed at jokes I didn't think were funny. I tried my best to half-ass my way through the night until a girl I've never seen before came up.

"This is all so stupid," was her opener. Got my attention immediately. We introduced ourselves; she explained her best friend works here, and she was brought along to not let her jump on some guy. When I asked where her friend was, she laughed and said probably jumping on some guy; she lost her over an hour ago. We had a pleasant conversation. It was nice to talk about something light. Lately, all the conversations I have are very dense and serious. It felt good to just talk about nothing of importance. I enjoyed it until she asked if I wanted to leave with her. "We could use the guise of love to get the hell out of here." She rolled her eyes at the word love.

This was a pivotal choice, I could tell. Because if I say sure, then I was basically saying that I was available. And I don't know if I actually am. I really truly don't know. But on the other hand, this party was so dull and draining I would have chewed my own arm off to leave.

So, I went out with her. We went to her car, and she drove me to mine. I like her; she is smart, easy to talk to, quick wit, good sense of humor. I really think we could be friends until she leaned in. I stopped her. I didn't know what I'm doing. Or what I want. I do know that I don't want to do anything I'll regret. I'm still all over the place. And I don't need to go pulling someone else into this mess. She gave me her number, and I might call. Like I said, I liked talking to her. I think it was also I liked the guy she saw me as. I wasn't the dying guy, I wasn't the widow guy, I wasn't fucked up, I wasn't a swirling vortex of indecision and anxiety, I was just a dude. I kind of liked that feeling. But then the logic sets in. She would get to know me and learn all those things. And if she has half a brain, run away screaming. I don't really know. And I know I say that a lot. But that's just honestly where I am at. I feel like my life is a question mark. The world is a question mark. I am a question mark. A living, breathing, question mark.

And I literally feel like I don't know anything at all. But I do know a few things. I know I miss Penny, I know that I feel like I'm dying, I know that I am one fucked up individual. And I know that I can't even think about kissing anyone until I figure out just what the actual fuck is going on.

Sincerely,
Not Sitting in a Tree

February 24

Shit. It's been a minute. Sorry. Where did I leave off? Valentine's Day, right? That girl I met; well, her name is Aubree. She's super cool; we have been hanging out a lot. Not dating, no funny stuff, just "talking," as the kids call it nowadays.

I enjoyed spending time with her. But I didn't quite know how to handle her. She wasn't sunshine like Penny, but she also didn't have ice in her veins like Nat. It was an odd endeavor; I have fallen for both sides of a coin. I've belonged to a heart of gold and fallen for a frost-bitten one; I didn't know what to do with a normal human heart.

Until I realized what I had to do: break it before it shatters. The realization came when we went to a movie. Stupid cheesy romcom. She was going on and on about the main guy the love he had for the girl. She liked how "real" it was, that it wasn't all grand gestures and roses. It was raw, emotional, and the bad times showcased the love better than the good. Yeah, I know; she's got a good head on her shoulders. But I was reaching for her door handle, and she unknowingly closed the chamber on any idea of "us."

"Have you ever loved someone like that?"

I froze. Completely. My brain stopped, heart felt like a jackrabbit in my chest. I tried to play it cool, but my face must have given it away.

"You have!" she squealed, all wide-eyed and interested. I laughed and walked around to my side, hoping that distance was enough to change the subject. It wasn't. She rapid-fired questions. "Who is she?" "Did she break your heart?" "Did you break hers?" "What happened?" She was so excited. I warned her with my eyes, half not ready to have this conversation, half jumping at the chance to talk about Penny.

"I... She.... Is... was... my wife... she... died," I stumbled over every single word. I finally looked up from the steering wheel. I don't know what I was expecting. Jealousy? Anger? That trademark "you poor thing" head tilt? But instead, she smiled and asked me to tell her everything. I didn't think she was serious, but she insisted.

So, I did. The whole drive home, this woman sat and listened to my favorite love story. She laughed at how we met. She shook her head in disbelief at the proposal. Remind me; I'll tell you those stories sometime. I showed her the paint stain tattoo that was my wedding band. I told her how Penny begged me not to let her paint the week before the wedding because it always stained her hands. I told her that she might as well tattoo a paint stain because she wouldn't be herself without paint on her hands. It was one of those lightbulb moments; we both had the same idea. We put up a canvas and painted. It was a thunderstorm on a lake, lots of grays and blues, and of course little yellow flowers all around. We ended up on the floor half-naked with paint everywhere. But then we each picked a mark on the other's right hand. Both blue. We threw on some clothes, went into a walk-in tattoo shop, and got that mark tattooed on our left ring finger. Our wedding bands. We didn't tell anyone until the actual wedding day. There was a lot of hand-holding and shoving them in couch cushions.

I told Aubree all of it. And it was bittersweet. On the one hand, I had missed telling these stories. But on the other, it felt weird telling it by myself. Like I was reading my lines, but the other half of the script went unsaid. But I just went with it, let it all come pouring out. I took a girl I'd known two weeks and sliced my chest open, right in front of her.

That's when it hit me. She was incredible. Here she was listening to this guy she barely knows ramble about how much he loves another woman. And that flipped me like a red light; she cared. She liked me. She cared about me; she was investing herself in me. And I can't keep her.

She isn't going to be the love of my life. But she sure as hell would be someone else's. This wasn't a one-night stand girl or a call-when-you're-bored-girl. This was the type of girl you marry. This is the kind of girl you let yourself, love.

I could never give her that with me dying. I didn't want to give her a chance. I figure I'll throw her overboard in a life jacket instead of letting her get sucked up in the sinking ship. So, I told her that we couldn't see each other anymore. She immediately got upset, saying she can wait, that there is no rush, we could just be friends.

"We have all the time in the world." Oh, darling, you have no idea that your world is going outlast mine.

I tried to explain myself, saying I'm not what she wants. To which she accused me of not knowing what she wants, which honestly was a good point, but I couldn't risk her lying. So, I told her that she would understand someday. I've already had my fairytale, and if anyone was ever going to get two in one lifetime, it's not me.

Then I had a really Mr. Poetic Pants moment and my brain somehow concocted this statement:

"I may deserve to be loved the way I love you, but you deserve to be loved the way I love her."

Yep. God damn. No idea where that shit came from, but I meant every word of it. She looked disappointed, but I think on some level, she knew I was right. Even though she didn't quite know why, I imagine it felt like letting a car pass you on the interstate. You don't know why your speed wasn't fast enough, but you just hope the driver gets where they are going safely. At least that's what I hope it felt like.

Anyway, I kissed her cheek and wished her the best. And again, I meant every damn word. I hadn't felt this much in a while. I had gotten so used to being an icebox of emotions. I drove home and, for the first time in months, felt certain. For the first time in a while, I didn't question a decision I made. I didn't wonder if I did the right thing. I know I did. This ship is going down, by bullet or by the ocean; it's going down. The less people on it, the better. I need to just do this on my own, whatever the fuck "this" ends up being.

So, you know how everyone has that one "thing" that you feel like it almost defines you? That one thing that everyone who meets you needs to know? You know what I'm talking about? Well, anyway, Penny is mine. She is the love of my life. No one will ever compare to her. No one will ever know me the way she did. I will never love anyone that way, so why even try?

Sincerely,
Mr. New Thing

March 1

Let me ask you something. What would you do if you were dying? If you had a few months or maybe a year to live, what would you do? Seriously. Think about it. Don't give me some bullshit answer. Sit down and think of the idea of you not being alive. Think about your family clutching your picture staring at a wooden box you've never seen. What the fuck would you do? What would you say? Would you spill everything you've got inside? Shout it from a rooftop, paint it on a billboard, publish a book and pray to God the right ears listen. If you realized you were dying, what would you do?

More importantly, how would you feel? What emotions would be in pulsating in your heart? Would you feel lonely? Scared? Angry? Confused? Or would you just kind of daze your way through? Because I think I'm more the latter. I don't know when this big life-ending thing is going to hit. I don't know what to do if it does. But I also don't know what to do until it does. Like, I just am kind of waiting for it. I don't know what I am supposed to do.

So, I thought I would go talk to the one person that might know. I decided it was time to go see Penny's grave. That maybe I was ready for it. That maybe if I could will myself out of the car, I might find a tiny speck of peace that I could hold onto. So, I went. And guess what? They wouldn't let me in. Some trucks crashed, and they wouldn't let anyone in. I tried. I wanted to kill the fake security guard. I mean, it would be the perfect place to kill someone. I mean, who is going to look for a dead body... in a cemetery? I pulled the "my wife died" card, I pulled the "I am dying" card, I pulled every card I had but to no avail.

   So, I don't know what to do. I've got the list on the fridge. But I am starting to lose faith in that too. Like, what is the point? It won't bring her back. What the hell am I supposed to do? And since I can't get to her, I figured maybe you would know. So, I apologize for the amount of question marks, but that's honestly a summary of where I am at.

Sincerely,
?????????

March 14

I am so screwed. I can't win, dude. I can't escape. Everything reminds me of Penny. Sunflowers and rainstorms. How can two things so contradictory remind me of the same person? Bright yellow and mind-numbing gray? Sprout up from the ground and pour down from the sky. Two different worlds braided into one beautiful soul. In case you couldn't tell by now, this is going to be a whiny, dramatic, Mr. Poetic Pants moment.

It's ironic how I've been brainwashed. Most people hate rainy days; they get all lonely and sad. But I am sadder on the sunny ones. Rainy days have always been good for me. Well, with Penny at least.

I guess I should have known things with her would be different when I met her in the middle of a fucking hurricane. She came into the bar I was working at, completely soaked. Her dark hair was stiff and dripping onto the floor. Her pantsuit clung to every part of her; she said she felt like she was wearing a leotard.

"Vodka sprite splash of cranberry with a lime." She apologized for the complicated order. I didn't have the heart to tell her I'd made that drink no less than 5,000 times. I played it cool and asked for her ID.

"Alright, Janine, here is your complicated order." I tried to be slick. All I got back was a glare.

"Don't call me that. It's Penny." She was already annoyed, and I'm sure some big goofy bartender hitting on her was not helping. But I luckily was either brave or stupid enough to ask if Penny was her middle name.

She told me it was her "chosen name." She launched into her whole life story pretty much. She left home as a teenager, had some family problems. Worked her ass off studying to be a lawyer. She had a long-time boyfriend, Rob. (I owe that poor bastard my life.) It was a comfortable relationship. Nothing exciting but the kind of love that was out of convenience instead of intent. She told me that she felt like she was sleepwalking through life. A zombie, not really living but not really dead. Relatable as hell right now.

But one night, she came home to find dozens of roses. There were candles and a stereo playing their song, and in the middle of the room, Rob was down on one knee. She was blindsided; she went from comfortably sleepwalking to wide awake and on the edge of a cliff. She asked for a minute and went out onto the balcony of their apartment. She truly did not know what to do or what she wanted. So, she being the crazy person she is, did the only thing she could think of: she flipped a coin. A Penny, to be exact. Heads: yes. Tails: no.

By the grace of every God that has existed, it was tails. So, she broke up with him, moved in with a friend, finished law school alone. The only person in the crowd for her at graduation was an old professor. She got an offer from a firm in Arizona, and now she was here. She went all the way down to the courthouse just to find the doors locked. She decided she needed a fucking drink and came to the only bar stupid enough to be open during a tropical storm.

And every single day, I silently thank my dickhead boss for being greedy enough to open. She and I sat for hours. Really got to know each other. Told childhood stories that in a few years, we'd have memorized. Eventually, the previously mentioned dickhead, said we were closing down.

Now I bet you are thinking this is perfect: lonely bartender gets off work early, beautiful stranger, pouring rain. Story writes itself. You've probably got that warm fuzzy feeling, don't you? I thought so too. I offered to walk her to her car down the street. We walked and got pelted by rain. I mean, we couldn't see two feet in front of us. I held the umbrella, but it blew backward no less than ten times. We made it to her car, and she quickly got in and said goodbye. That was it. No movie scene. No warm and fuzzies. Just cold, wet everything.

And my heart actually broke at the idea that those hazy taillights were the last I'd see her until I got to work the next day and found a phone with sunflowers on the case. My heart leaped at the possibility of it being hers. I called the emergency contact and talked to her friend Richard. She came in a few hours later, she hugged me and insisted she take me to dinner, which I found out years later was an excuse; she hadn't stopped thinking about me since she left. She even turned around at the light to see if I was still close, but I had already driven off. That time we did get our movie scene. Light sprinkle, quiet city, neon lights. Perfect first kiss. Fucking magic.

But yeah, anyway, the point is every major day of our relationship, it rained. We met: tropical storm. First kiss: sprinkle. First time we had sex: the storm of the century. Proposal: light rain. Wedding: downpour.

I just don't get how a person can represent two opposites so wonderfully. Half her clothes were pastel dresses and the other half was dark pantsuits. She was a strong, sturdy lawyer who used iron-clad words to argue for justice. But then she came home, let her hair down, and painted beautiful masterpieces. Left brain and right brain. Dull and shine. She was both sides of the coin every time. And goddamn, I fucking love her. Sunflowers and rainstorms. I fell in love with a walking contradiction. And now I'm screwed.

Sincerely,
Sad In Sunshine

April 3

There are two things I don't like talking about: my stupid grief club and my disease. Well, here is an update on both: they suck.

I've done some moderate treatment, basically pills and breathing into a tube. The doctors want to move on with more progressive measures. They haven't jumped on the train of lost hope I've been driving lately, but they are getting closer to the station for pick up.

I don't really care about treatment. Honestly, I don't care about anything at all. Just the list. That's the only thing going on in my mind. I moved it from the fridge to the mirror on the dresser. I see it every day. It's there, mocking my every move. I've only done one thing on it since I found it. Went to a play. Woo. Watching grown men in tights sing. Huge accomplishment, clearly.

The guilt has been really heavy on me lately and then at stupid grief club, the counselor who could not be more than 12 years old said something that struck me:

"You can't let the loss consume your life."

It took everything I had not to stand up and deck this freshman-looking mother fucker. How the hell am I supposed to do that? How is losing the love of your life not going to consume your life? Look, maybe Lil Troy Bolton over here didn't let the grief of Gabriella breaking his little wildcat heart consume his life. But there is no way this punk knows what it feels like to lose real love.

I mean, I live inside a giant shrine to our relationship. I eat the food we used to go halfsies on, I wrap myself in the towels we argued over, I buy the same brand of cotton swabs she likes out of habit. How the actual fuck can you tell me this isn't supposed to take me over? How can you sit there in your little khaki shorts and tell me that my life will be okay without her? How am I supposed to just move on? Burn the house down? Move away from everyone I know? Please, all-mighty Nickelodeon reject, tell me how you accept the concept that all of the memories you will ever have with someone are made. Tell me, please, if you've got all the answers in that Bitmoji head of yours. Give it up.

I wanted to say all that. Well, actually a much less thought out and much more profanity-filled version of that, but you get the point. But that did give me an idea. You know how sometimes someone says something so incredibly stupid you get a brilliant idea? That was this moment.

Bitmoji boy said, don't let it consume your life. But that is exactly what I am going to do. So, I quit my job. And treatment. And pretty much everything else. I quit playing pick-up hockey. I quit going out. Everything but family and the list. Those are the only things that I need to even be thinking of. There is no telling how much longer I've got on this bitch-ass planet, so I might as well do the things that matter. Fuck money, I can't bring that with me to the afterlife, nor the grave. I would rather reunite with my love with a handful of memories than a fist full of cash. Even if I only get to see her in passing. I want to be able to tell her it's done. We did it all. Let our story finish as wonderfully as we began. So that's the goal. The only goal from here on out.

Sincerely,
Full Time Quitter

April 6

    Alright, I actually have a free moment, and I have been meaning to tell you the proposal story. But this is an amazing story. My favorite stepping stone in our relationship, so I wanted to wait until I had time to truly do it justice.
    It was a Saturday morning, September 30th, to be exact. We were off work and decided to just take a day to relax. To breathe. We were living in an apartment on 5th floor of the building. We were out on the balcony, had just gotten out of the shower. It was warm but rainy. It was past sunrise, but just enough of it hanging in the sky to make everything look gold. She was on my lap, wearing the gray robe that was her first "big girl purchase" when she was 16. It was old and tattered, but she adored it. She had on blue slippers with sunflower buttons on them that Annalise had gotten her for Christmas. Her hair was still damp. Her skin was shiny from the vitamin whatever serum she used.
    Now I had an original plan for this huge grand romantic scene: fancy dinner, me in a tux, her in a satin dress. I even got my office building to allow my electrician friend to make a heart out of our lit-up windows. I went big. I planned to, at least. But sitting there, it just hit me. This was the moment. This summed us up better than anything. Real, natural, peaceful. This was the perfect snapshot of our relationship, and what better moment

to start the next chapter in. So, I excused myself. She laughed and asked if I had to poop. Teasing that my duces always ruin our romantic moments.

    I laughed too and made my way to the closet. Even went through the bathroom so she wouldn't suspect anything. I grabbed the ring and also my phone. Normally I try to stay off my phone in these kinds of moments; I mean, this one was monumental. The single most important question I'd ever ask. The answer would either make my life or burn it to the ground. But for some reason, I stopped, and I took a picture. Undeniably my favorite one ever. And I am so glad I did. It's one of my favorites. It was my lock screen for the entire engagement. I put the phone down, took a deep breath, (back when I could do that,) bent down on one knee and said her name trying not to let my voice or hands shake.

    She turned around, her smile dropped to the concrete, her eyes widened into golf balls. I was expecting a squeal or a jump or to be tackled to the ground, but before I could get past "will you-"

    She rushed past me, saying "hold on!"

    My heart stopped. I was petrified. The plan in my head, we were already kissing. Was this a "No."? Would I soon hear keys jingle and watch our finale end the same way we began: with taillights fading into the storm?

    She came running back holding a picture frame. It used to hang on the wall in the hallway to the laundry room. It was her in front of Mt. Rushmore. She had short hair that ran slightly past her shoulders when it was down. But it was pulled up in a bun that poked out of this capless beanie thing. It poked out like a dark little puffball. Neon pink puffy jacket, dark jeans, and yellow rain boots. The leaves all around her were orange and crisp, like they would definitely crunch when stepped on. I knew this photo very well; it was taken two days after she left Rob. She drove 18 hours straight and ended up there. That was the birth of "Penny" as we knew her.

She held the edges of the frame delicately, glancing it over for what felt like an eternity. Then threw it as hard as she could at the wall directly behind me. Missing my head by only a foot.

"Damn. A simple 'no' would have sufficed." I started to stand up, feeling as shattered as the glass.

"No! No! No!" She stepped closer, pushing me back on one knee.

"Just wait! Hold on!" She started picking up handfuls of the glass and splinters and suffering a few minor slices.

"Ahha! Give me your hand!" she grabs my wrist, cupping her entire hand around mine. I feel something drop onto my palm. I open it and see a penny. My head, still swirling, doesn't comprehend.

"Don't you see? It's *THE* penny." She started to tear up. I just nodded, unsure of the critical puzzle piece I was missing in this situation.

"And it's on heads." She smiled coyly, slightly proud of her genius.

"Sooo, is that a yes?" I chose my words carefully, as if I was coaxing a horse into a stable. One wrong word, and she would outrun Sea Biscuit.

104

"Exactly. But see, this time, I'm not leaving it up to fate. I am choosing you. Not because of luck or the universe or some deity told me to because I want to. Purposely. Intentionally. Eternally. Choosing you over fate."

I was speechless. The only human being on this planet that could make the answer to a proposal more beautiful than the proposal itself. Damn, she was incredible. I mean, I know that everyone says their wife or partner is astonishing. But like mine seriously was. She wasn't amazing because I loved her; I loved her because she was amazing.

She radiated love and life and happiness. But she was realistic and grounded, so you never felt like you were having a conversation with a Hallmark movie script. She cared for others; she was never afraid to stand up for what she believed in, and even when she was; she did anyway. She was everything anyone should ever want to be. Maybe that's why she died so young. She had life figured out.

How the hell I got the chance to share my life with her, I don't know. But the relief washed over me when she said yes. Goddamn. Our entire relationship, I was always scared she would run. She'd change her mind or realize I'm not good enough and catch the next flight before I even made it home. But this. This was a pact. A pinky promises on steroids. A commitment. No more winds to catch. No more fading taillights. No more coin flips. She swore she'd never leave me. And through no fault of her own, she did.

Sincerely,
Broken Picture Frame

April 15

Second box checked! I flew in one of those helicopters in the Grand Canyon. Despite living in Arizona, I'd only been there like twice. Everyone I know thought of it as touristy, the same way people who live in Florida don't go to Disney world every weekend.

Which they aren't wrong. There were hundreds of people. To be fair, it is springtime and the perfect time to go to the desert. But riding through it was one of those "down the road" ideas Penny and I had. Ya know, the kind that is like "when we have the money," "when we have vacation days," "when the weather was right, and we didn't have Suzy whatsherface's wedding." We always found an excuse not to do it. But I am not making any excuses anymore. I'm going to sound like a huge bowl of cliche cheese flakes, but seriously life is too fucking short not to do whatever the fuck you want to do. Did swearing un-cheese it up? Regardless, cliches are cliches for a reason.

So, I went on the ride, went to the little booth thingy, swiped my credit card for I don't even care how much, and went to the safety briefing. Half ass listened to all the things that could go wrong, the literal dozens of ways I could die. I didn't care at first, but then I thought of the pilot. I should pay attention just in case he doesn't want to die. So, I listened; I already knew the majority of the things covered, and I hoped that if something did go wrong, my brain would remember all the training I've had bulldozed into my skull.

Ten minutes later, we were in the air. And let me tell you something, it was breathtaking. The way the rocks swirled, looking like a Carmel sundae a 5-year-old made. Sometimes I forget how amazing nature is, then I get starstruck at the concepts and processes going on every single second. I start thinking about the way the oceans are controlled by a giant floating rock 200 thousand miles from here. I think about trees adjusting to seasons, letting go, in the hopes of blooming again. I think about all the things we humans don't know. All the existences we don't understand or merely don't know about. The wolves know what the moon is. The octopus learns how to open doors and latches. The way clouds and water randomly start twisting and turning in the middle of the ocean. The way a river runs into a rock until it dissolves it. I get blown away by all the incredible things in this thing we call life. And then I wonder why the hell we get so hung up on the little things. We freak out, overexpressing feelings and paying taxes. It's ridiculous.

Anyway, that was almost a good transition to what I really came to talk about. The helicopter dropped me off in this little landing inside the canyon. I didn't quite know what to do for the 30-minute break. I took a few pictures, mostly for Lise and Mom. I found two rocks wedged together, and I stuck a sunflower in it. I decided that would be a nice way to have her here with me. Something that isn't permanent, it's not hazardous to wildlife or the environment. But just a little note to the world from me and my love. And then I just sat there. On the ground and I felt calm, a feeling I had become a stranger to. And sitting there feeling the warm rock underneath me, the cool air, the sun barely making its way down to me, my mind replayed a message my mom had given me decades ago.

"Every life is like a grade level in school, each time, it gets harder because you use what you learned in your past lives even when you don't realize it."

It threw me for a loop; I hadn't thought of that concept in years. Literally, since I had been an adult, but it led me to something, and you are the only one I could bother with this kind of stuff, so here is my theory.

Alright, let's start this with the basic concept of multiple lives as well as the existence of heaven and hell. Now hear me out, but I don't believe that people who commit suicide go to hell. Because in our little analogy here, that is the equivalent of failing a class. God isn't a bad parent; in fact, He's the only perfect one to ever exist. So, he isn't going to send his child to hell because the pain was too much for them. He'll let them rest and then send them to do it again. Obviously not with the same people or even in the same time period but the same lessons. So, when you actually think about it, suicide isn't an escape or even a pause in life. It's a reset button. And yeah, that may sound appealing but think about all the heartache you've been thru. ALL of it. Every tear you've cried, every love you've lost, everything from not getting a Valentine in 3rd grade to putting the love of your life in the ground. If you kill yourself, then that doesn't mean the pain goes away; it means it RESTARTS. You will have to do it all over again. You have to lose more love, get more hurt, do everything you are supposed to learn how to deal with all over again. So, when you actually think about it, the best way to get as little pain as possible is to live through it.

A tangent of that theory is the idea of helpers. The "old souls," the ones here to teach us, newbies, the ropes. Like in elementary school when they brought in 7th graders to teach us multiplication tables. It wasn't just to give the teachers a break, the older ones got the experience of teaching, and the younger ones got a better understanding. Which this would explain "the good ones die young." Because they aren't meant to be here that long, they come into our classroom, teach us for a bit until we can somewhat do it on their own. And then they go back to their own learning. Their own lives. And we only get them for a fleeting moment.

I realize I probably sound batshit crazy and very, very hypocritical. But I can't help it; the past two days, my brain has been on this conquest and keeps coming up with these grand ideas. But I'm not too farfetched. You know? Haven't you ever felt deja vu? Or navigated a band new situation because you somehow just "knew" what to do? Haven't you ever had a friend that opened their mouth and a Greek philosopher came out? You're just sitting there like, dude, I just watched you order a McChicken in a Darth Vader voice how the fuck are you the same person? Like all these little things that are painting a bigger picture is the only explanation for. I don't know if I'm on to something or just losing my mind. Or shit, maybe they are one and the same. Lord knows historically genius people are crazy. Not that I'm a genius, but these thoughts I'm having do seem to make sense. Ha. Maybe I should write a book.

        Sincerely,
        Life Explained by the Dying (Damn, that would be a good title)

April 17

Love is booze.

Souls drink shit

Old souls

New souls

    Okay. Good morning. Ha-ha, the above is drunk me trying to explain a theory. I'm in Los Angles right now; since Penny wasn't specific about what she wanted to do here, I've done it all pretty much. Walk of Fame. Shopped in Beverley Hills. Bought an ice cream just to say I bought something. Went on the hike where you can see the Hollywood sign. That's where I left the sunflower for this box.

    I had an unrealistic fantasy about being famous. I drove past all the mansions and Ferraris, dreaming of swimming in pools of money. But then I realized I would be so lonely. I mean, what is the point of a real marble floor if your footsteps are the only ones it hears? Is it worth it? Fame is such an interesting concept. People get rich by getting other people to pay to hear or see them. I don't get it. Plus, then there is no privacy.

everyone always knowing everything. And if they don't, they make it up and sell the story anyway. I am not sure I would want that. Would you? Or let me put it this way, I wouldn't want to be that kind of famous. Now, if I did something wonderful and people poured a million dollars into a GoFundMe for me... That kind I would be okay with.

But anyway, I am getting off track. I went out last night, not sure why I didn't just stay in the hotel room, but I ended up meeting this group of people. Somehow on a rooftop bar. I think I'm not really sure. I don't remember much except asking a girl to get off my lap and then trying really hard to calculate a tip. Think I took a cab? Maybe I walked? Could I have died? Been mugged? Murdered? Lost forever in a city I don't know? Yes. Did I? Nope. Somehow, I made it back to my hotel in the correct room and even relocked the door. I'm not really sure when I made it back, but when I did, I scribbled this concept down. And this morning, I found cocktail napkins covered in more references and examples. Because apparently, I am that guy now, the one that does homework at a party. But anyway, as per usual, you're the only one I can bother with the shit, so here we go. Because believe it or not, I think drunk me had some solid points.

I was at the bar, and it must have been a couple's night or something because I swear everyone was with someone. And I noticed that you could practically tell how committed each of them was. How happy they were. It got me thinking about the different kinds of love, more specifically, the different levels. Well, the life of the party-me got to thinking and scribbling, and this is what he's got so far:

We've already established that souls come back, and the older souls get more difficult lessons. Now let's replace that word difficult with something more positive, like complex, evolved, or advanced. Then wouldn't it make sense that the loves they know and the lessons that come with them would be as evolved/complex/advanced? So, let's put this into a context we all can understand: alcohol. Yes, I was intoxicated, and it was on my mind, but hear me out.

Think back to when you were 16; I'm willing to bet you believed the whole world revolved around you. Everything you did was to learn who you were, how to take care of yourself, and how to be a member of society. (Lots of bullshit in society, but we can discuss that later.) New souls are the same way; they are learning how to be human, how to live and what feelings are.

So now put yourself in God's shoes; you have this brand new, acne-faced, geeked-up nerd child of a soul that wants to learn about love. The same thing as a 16-year-old asking for their first drink. You wouldn't hand that motherfucker a jar of moonshine and say good luck, kiddo. Right? No, you start them off easy; wine, beer, one of those pussy boy spritzer things. Something with enough alcohol that they feel the buzz but not enough to hurt them.

Life does the same thing. It wants to introduce us to "true love" damn, I hate saying that I feel like a fucking cartoon mouse. But anyway, it doesn't want us to get hurt right off the bat. Because it may be the greatest buzz you've ever felt, but that just means it's the worst hangover when it ends. Life knows this, so it gives the newer ones easier hangovers. They get "wine-drunk-love." You know the type. They met as teenagers, love at first sight, no cheating, no abuse, living the perfect Instagramable life. From the outside, looking in wine-drunk, love looks pretty good. But you have to take into consideration; the wine only takes you so far. The connection only goes so deep, most of the time not even to the soul level, because the newbies don't know how to defend their energy yet. So, they have a sweet-tasting buzzed but still sober kind of love.

    Then think about us older souls. The ones that crave something deeper, as they have built up a tolerance to unfulfilling surface connections. It no longer excites them. And let me tell you, nothing is more frustrating than sitting at the bar of life and feeling like the bartender is purposely ignoring you. Standing in suits watching friend after friend giggly as they sip from an overflowing wine river while you are sitting there stone cold sober.

    Funny thing is I always thought there was something wrong with me because I wasn't being served. I thought that maybe I didn't deserve to be drunk. That I made some awful decision and my entire love life was the repercussion of that. But damn, was I wrong. There was a reason I never got handed a wine glass. There was a reason the bartender didn't look my way. Because there was a beautiful dark-haired goddess who loved thunderstorms and sunflowers and F,R,I,E,N,D,S, and knee-socks on her way with a bottle of whiskey, that ended up being stronger than 12 of those wine girls combined. Part of me wishes that I could go back and tell that guy what he's got coming. But then that brings up the whole-time traveler paradox, where if I told him the future, it would change it. I was always so sure I didn't want to know. My entire life, I would ramble on about how life is all about the journey. And it's true, but you don't realize it until the journey is ending. Maybe I've been way off base all this time. Would you want to know? If someone came to you and said, I can show you your future, would you sneak a peek? I guess it depends on the person, but I have always answered that question with a no. But now, honestly, I would still say no but instead, ask how long I've got left. I don't care about what happens, who shows up; I know everything is going to work out like it is supposed to, but I just want to know when. That's me though; I am the guy that hits a scary part in a book and flips to see how many pages I've got left. Or pauses a movie during a plot twist to make sure there is enough time to get things resolved. I don't care what happens, just when. And in a crude sense of irony, the guy who finds comfort in timelines no longer has one. Add it to the list of lessons, I guess.

So anyway, that's my theory; souls get different levels of love based on how their age and experience. Whatever the universe knows, they can handle. So, I guess it's good news no matter where you land on that scale.

Because if you're a wine drinker, then your loves will be happy and simple and lovely. If you're a whiskey drinker, then you get a nice deep buzz. And if you haven't ever had a drop in your life, that means you've probably got a really fucking good shot coming your way. And it will change you, down to your being. And I'm here to tell you even with the god-awful, heart-shattering hangover, it's worth it. Every time.

Sincerely,
Whiskey Drinker

April 19

Another box checked! Joshua Tree National Park. I never really understood the hype over this place. I always thought it was just a desert, nothing special. But let me tell you this place is breathtaking. There is this weird, sinky, touchy sand. All these huge, peculiar scratchy rocks that look like they were God's building blocks, and he got called in for dinner. Thrown and stacked haphazardly yet perfectly. Then the Joshua trees. I never thought I would love a spiky, shaggy, willy wonka-looking tree, but I did! It was beautiful. The mountains, the cacti, the trees and rocks, and the sand. It was all beautiful by its own definition.

I climbed onto the top of this one stack and was blown away by the view. Something out of a brochure that makes you go, "Oh, that has to be photoshopped." Nope. Nothing fake out here. I sat on the edge for a while, ate a sandwich, and laid the sunflower next to me. Obviously, I missed Penny, found myself wishing she was there, but oddly enough, my brain didn't stop there.

I started missing everyone. It was like I got throat punched by this wave of emotion. One of those pauses in the Matrix moments when it hits you? You become incredibly aware of everything, your existence, the love you have for people, the thoughts you have. Like your entire being goes into a hyperactive mode, and you can't stop feeling a wave of gratitude for whatever it is you are most thankful for. You ever had one of those moments?

    I hadn't had one of those moments in years. But yet here it was. I suddenly wished everyone I loved was here, not just Penny. I wanted to watch my Dad snapping pictures of every plant and bug so he could google them when he got phone service. I wished that I could see my mom and grandma stuffing her pockets with rocks. I would give anything to watch my sister get frustrated over not being able to get the perfect family photo. Michael and I would be racing, making contests over who jumped off the highest rock. Annalise would climb to the top of a cliff and take a nap. Penny most definitely would have run to the car, grabbed her "emergency" paint set, and started painting away. She'd paint this unbelievable landscape, and then we'd hang it in the living room with the others, cementing it into her personal Wall of Fame. I even thought of you. I wondered what you would do, whose lead would you follow? I don't know, but I almost wish I could. I wish I could just wiggle my nose and bring you all here. Just keep everyone in this happy, safe, very hot but peaceful land. Make a giant bubble, and we all would live here forever. Maybe the heat has gotten to me, but at the moment, it sounded nice. It felt nice. And I haven't had a lot of nice feelings lately, so I'll take it.

                                      Sincerely,
                                      Sending Mental Postcards

May 15

I recognize it's been a few weeks; honestly, I relapsed a little bit. I went home after Joshua Tree, and I just crashed. Turned my phone off, laid in bed watching mindless TV. I lost my focus, I lost my edge.

But I am back, and I'm on a plane to New York. The list specifically says the Statue of Liberty, but I've never been, so I have wanted to do all the touristy stuff. Penny loved New York; I guess she went when she had her little "who am I?" adventure after Rob. She always talked about going back. She always wanted to take me, but we never found the time. And stupid us thought we'd have more of it. But anyway, I'm actually really excited about this trip.

It's a long flight to JFK, and I've never been able to sleep on a civilian plane. I'm not sure if it's the height or my neck at an awkward part of the seat or my legs cramped. I don't know, but I can't sleep.

So, I've been thinking about a lot of things, and one of the thoughts I ended up coming back to is the whole Love to Alcohol Theory. And I think I may have just discovered another level of it. Or at least a tangent. If we continue on the base premise of different levels of love and our previous theory that souls learn lessons at increasing levels of difficulty, it's possible that these two go hand in hand. What if instead of just being on a whiskey level love, we are actually on a whiskey level life? All or at least the majority of our lessons would be (on a grander scale) relatively equal. This would also confirm the idea of Karma. What comes around goes around. If you get hit with the really bad shit, you've got really good shit coming your way. This is basically one large theory broken down to be better understood. At least it's broken down for me. But what I realized is that these different life and love levels might actually be able explain some of the more "human" parts of love/relationships.

For example, cheating. The instance that came to my mind was a couple I knew in college, Noah and Tyra. Noah was a very deep minded, open-hearted, genuine dude. He lost his Dad when he was young, had multiple life failures, battled alcohol addiction, and both completely lost and found God. Pretty heavy stuff. He's good; I'll say a "Jack Honey level," dude. Then, on the other hand, Tyra was an airhead trust fund baby who spent her entire life eating off her Father's or Daddy's silver spoon. The worst loss she had ever suffered was burying a 25-cent goldfish. Seriously she told me that at a party one time. Needless to say, it's safe to be she's newer to the game; I'll be nice and say she's hard lemonade.

So, we have a sweet whiskey boy and a hard lemonade girl. What happens when you love someone? You exchange energy. That's like the whole point, right? Love is energy. Connection is energy. Our boy Noah is giving Tyra some decently strong love shots. She's good and plastered, touring churches and flipping through bridal magazines. And she is giving him everything she has, but everything she has is hard lemonade. Now any drinker knows, hell, I'm sure even non-drinkers know, that it's going to take a lot of hard lemonade to get you even CLOSE to the level of drunk you get off a good, double charcoaled bourbon. Eventually, Noah realizes that he doesn't feel what he expected to; he tried to rectify it. He put in more effort. He listened and planned romantic dates. He did everything he could to feel a buzz from her, but at the end of the day, it just wasn't enough.

And that's when his male human brain kicked in, and, like most men, he convinced himself that he could fill any gap in his life with his dick. So, he cheated.

He felt awful afterward. We were all shocked. He was such a good guy, they had the "perfect" relationship, but at the end of the day, she wasn't enough for him. Now here is the shitty thing: she didn't do anything wrong. She didn't drive him away. She didn't make him feel unwanted. She did nothing but love him with every cell of her tiny brained body. But they just weren't a match. As humans, we have an obsession with closure. With certainties and all "why's" answered. But sometimes, it just is because it is. This was one of those cases.

But like I said, everything evens out. Tyra ended up finding someone on her level; they are intoxicatingly happy living a simple life together. And she met him because of Noah's friend. So, it all happened for the right reason, but in the end, she needed to find someone who matched her energy. And so, did he.

That, I think, is part of the challenge, finding someone who drinks the same love you do. We look at all the human aspects of compatibility: age, geography, love language, astrological signs, personality tests. But we fail to consider the compatibility of our inner beings if we have corresponding purposes, or similar life lessons, or at the very least, lessons in the same range so that we know how to understand each other and our reactions.

I think that would be a good way to start weeding out potential loves. Not for me obviously, I had my perfect buzz. But you get what I am saying. Because when we end up in uneven energy exchange, our human sides take over. And we fuck it up. Or at least we think we fuck it up.

That's a hard concept to swallow, but I think it's one worth talking about. Now I am in no way condoning adultery. But maybe cheater Noah wasn't a bad guy after all; he was just doing what he was meant to. Just some thoughts that have been rumbling around this crazy cranium of mine.

Sincerely,
Mile High Thoughts

May 16

    First day in New York. Penny was completely right; this place is its own kind of magical. There is this weird vibe. I was used to cities, but this one was just unique. I got into my hotel late, so my introduction to Times Square was at night, which is a tricky statement because it wasn't dark at all. It was glowing and alive with the light of every neon color you could think of. No wonder this city never sleeps. Everything is crystal clear; despite everything being so smashed and crammed, there are solid defined edges to everything. It's a whirlwind of colors and faces and buildings that make the world feel bigger than you. The kind of feeling you had when you were a kid, and even your parents seemed larger than life. I miss life feeling like that. Being enamored by existing, just seeing everything as the wonderment it is.

    This city gives me that feeling. I am actually very excited to play tourist tomorrow and see more of it. I'm just giving in to any feeling at this point. I'm too tired to argue or rationalize with them. So, if my brain wants to run around with stars in my eyes snapping pictures like a tourist and not giving a single fuck who is watching. Guess what I am going to do? That.

    I am enjoying this not caring about anything attitude. Not giving a fuck is an odd but very valid version of peace. I'm sure I will tell you all about it. But I just wanted to update you on where I am at. I'm feeling okay at the moment, almost like a part of me belongs here. Penny always said that. That it wasn't fully home, but it felt like a piece of her was made for this city. I'm really starting to understand what she meant. And I just got here. Ha. So, this should be interesting.

Sincerely,
New Found New Yorker

May 17

Here's the thing, I love talking to you, I do. But I am falling apart. So, I need to talk to my wife. I've tried praying or just talking out loud, but I don't feel it, I don't feel anything, and I really really need to, so for the next few minutes, I need the "you" to be Penny. Okay? I'm sorry.

How? How can you possibly be everywhere? I'm in a city you've been to ONCE. A city thousands of miles away from our home, and yet you are still here. Lingering around as if the entire world has just been dusted in you.

There are other hands in the world, I know that. Logically I know that, but how come every damn pair I see is yours? Somehow the pictures on the billboards are your hands. The waitress at the restaurant has them too. I can't tell you how many steps in the wrong direction I've taken because I saw long dark hair flowing in the breeze. How many times I've had to remind my brain to ignore the instinct to chase anything that looks like you or feels like you or smells like you or reminds me of one thing you did one time. I see bits of you. The waitress had your hands. The hotel clerk had a freckle on the inside of her elbow. I've seen your sunflower tattoo on a girl in a movie. I see your eyes in the kid selling lemonade in California. I've heard your laugh playing like a stuck record, and I'm never sure if it's in my head.

It's like when you died; God divided you up. Took all the traits and quirks and beautiful pieces of you and gave them away.

To everyone except me. They get your hands, your eyes, your tattoo, your walking movements. They roam this planet, having no idea that they have pieces of the most incredible soul to ever exist. They have you, and they don't care. And yet, I'm here with nothing but fading memories and a dry toothbrush I don't have the heart to throw out.

    Here I am, begging for moments to remember, staring at the sky, bargaining with my own breath for pieces of you. But you keep escaping me. Disappearing at a glance's notice. Like your ghost is attracted to everyone except the one who loves you most. It's like we are strangers again. And the worst part isn't the loss of you. It is seeing you. It's the similarities that make my brain forget you're gone. It's the 0.0001 seconds of hope and joy that is ripped away faster than a blink. The crash after that, that's the worst part. How the hell am I supposed to accept you being gone when I see you everywhere but with me? Why do random waitresses and models get to be so lucky to have a part of you? Why don't I? Was I not good enough to be in the line? Was my love not enough to purchase an eternal piece of you? I thought we agreed we were forever. Till death do us part is for fucking quitters. It was supposed to be you and me till the end of time. But the clocks are still ticking. The Earth is still spinning, and somehow, I have nothing left of you.

    Sincerely,
    I Love You but You Are Killing Me

May 19

I am going to finish telling you about the New York trip, but I would like to thank you first. Thank you for letting me talk to Penny. I didn't realize how angry I was. I didn't even know I was mad at her, which makes no sense, but according to this giraffe video on the internet about the stages of grief, it is normal. It honestly felt good to see my words instead of feeling them falling out of my mouth invisibly. I could almost feel her looking over my shoulder; granted, those aren't exactly the prettiest or sweetest words, but they are the words I needed her to hear.

So anyway, New York. It was a fun trip. I did all the normal touristy stuff. I rode to the top of the Freedom Tower. I cried at Ground Zero. I bought the family a bunch of cliche souvenirs; I heart NY stuff. Got my mom an M+M mug. Got Michael a fake Lady Liberty. Ha, I guess I don't really need to say fake, huh? Like, oh yeah, I took the real one. Just packed that shit in my carry-on.

The last stop was the Empire State Building. Penny had told me of the view and made me swear I would never Google pictures so that I could "genuinely experience it." She also said it's much better at night. So, I waited till the last hour they were open. No line breezed right in. I stopped only a few times to read some of the posted museum pieces. I got into the elevator and felt my heart begin to race. It was a feeling I'd never felt, the air grew crisper like the kind you feel at the top of a mountain, but it got there quicker. It was cold, I had a slight chill underneath my sleeves, and it was moving so fast. It was like the entire world was on a crescendo, just building up and up and up. Then the doors opened. I went out to the railing, and once again, my love was right.

The view was incredible; the entire city lit up like Christmas time in the middle of spring. The cars slide along like a child's matchbox toys. Even through the very tall chain link fence on top of the railing, I could see thousands of windows flickering like fireflies. It was incredible to think that all of the people in those windows existed. Each of them having their own beautiful, complex, crazy life. They all have problems and happiness and feelings and thoughts, and yet to me; they are nothing but a window light. I got so lost in this idea and the view I didn't realize a teenage girl had made her way next to me.

"If you could have dinner with anyone dead or alive, who would it be?"

That was her opener. I jumped, slightly startled as I had fully intended not having any conversations up here. She was this cute little punk-looking kid. Bright pink hair, a couple of piercings, tattoos, ripped jeans, and a black shirt. She looked like the typical rebellious phase in a person. I asked her why she was asking.

She shrugged and offered me a cigarette. I thought about taking it for a second, but I decided against it.

"I like to know one random thing about strangers. You know? Kind of like a collection. A tidbit of information from someone you will never see again."

I don't know what answer I was expecting, but it wasn't that. I was intrigued by the concept, though. Imagine having hundreds of stories with no beginning or endings. Little mental snapshots with no context, just standing alone. I was honored to be a part of it. I told her I needed a second to think about who my dinner guest would be.

My first thought was Penny, but then I realized I had dinner with her hundreds of times. If I got to have one truly magically dinner, I would probably pick my Grandpa on my dad's side. He was a good ole' fashioned tough-as-nails American badass. The kind they don't really make anymore. WWII vet and then construction worker after that.

My dad always told me there was nothing that man didn't know. Jack of all trades and keeper of all life's answers. He died when I was a very little kid. I have like one or two foggy memories of him; the rest of his image has been filled with stories I've heard. I feel like he would be a good person to have a conversation with.

Now that I'm an adult, we could sit down man to man. I'd ask about life. How to deal with the flashbacks. How to unsee things. Plus, he lost his first wife when he was younger; maybe he could tell me how to survive it. Maybe he could tell me it gets easier. Or he could tell me it doesn't. Tell me I should name the poking hot lump of coal that is constantly in my stomach because it isn't going anywhere.

Even if it wasn't the answers I wanted to hear, it would be nice to have any kind of guidance. So, I think he would be my choice.

I unloaded all of that on this poor kid. I felt better for a moment, like yet another weight I didn't realize I was carrying was off my shoulders. But then I felt guilty. This wasn't the time or place for that realization. This chick is just trying to be quirky, and I crashed onto her like a tidal wave. I expected her to walk away or laugh or just be like, "yeah, ok, bro, bye."

But she was unfazed. She stared out into the view, for a long moment and then in one motion hugged me. Just for a split second, then pulled away quickly.

"Well, Empire State Building Dude."

"My name is-" I tried to interject.

"La la la," She covered her ears. "Doesn't matter. To me, you will always be Empire State Building, dude. Anyway, I'll tell you this." She turned to make sure I was looking at her.

"It doesn't get easier, but it does get quieter. It won't always be this loud."

My eyebrows practically shot up into my hair. How did she know? Was she right? Who did she lose? Father? Mother? Sibling? Friend? Boyfriend? How could this literal child walking around at 10 p.m. hugging random strangers in the busiest city in America, know what loss was and how to deal with it?

I never got the chance to ask her. By the time I formulated any of those questions, she was in the elevator on her way down. Never learned her name or her story. She's just the girl from the Empire State Building.

It got me thinking how one question can open someone up like that. It was an interesting concept. For example, if I asked you who you would have dinner with, dead or alive, who would you say? 50/50 shot, you're either going to say some celebrity, or you're going to crack open like I did. She taught me something. And the crazy part is she's just a drifting moment. Like the firefly windows, a temporary existence in my reality. But one I will remember for the remainder of my life.

I don't know if there are such things as guardian angels. And if there are, I'm not sure they have pink hair and face piercings, but she gave me what I was looking for.

"It doesn't get easier, but it does get quieter."

But then again, I'll be dead soon anyway, and technically everything will be quiet. But until then, it's a nice fantasy to believe in.

Sincerely,
Empire State Building Dude

May 21

What is your most embarrassing memory? Go ahead take a second to think about it. For my whole life, my most embarrassing memory was my pants falling down during a middle school dance battle. But I am unhappy to say that moment has officially been dethroned, but I'll get to that.

First, I want to talk about words. Words. And how they suck. They are just letters and syllables put together. They shouldn't hold that much power. It's weird how they can feel different. For example, the word death feels heavier than the word life. Or the word "goodbye" is sadder than the word "bye." There is literally no difference. 4 letters. 4 letters spelling out a word that is normally seen as a positive somehow makes it sadder.

You never say "goodbye" to your friends when you leave a party. Or at the end of a nice date. You say "goodbye" to a dying being. You say "goodbye" to something that is hard to let go of. But then, on the flip side, if you say "good morning," that statement is somehow more upbeat and happier than just "morning." Exact same concept. The exact same word. Polar opposite results. And the craziest part is that it's just a known thing; we humans have created these unspoken known double meanings.

Anyway, words are stupid; that is my point. They are just letters. They shouldn't be able to break someone's heart. Or mend someone's scars. Or make a full-grown 34-year-old man yell at an innocent old lady on an airplane...

Yep, I was flying back home, and I had my laptop and The List on my tray table. I was researching and planning for the next trip. And this sweet old lady next to me started talking. Not minding her business like most old women don't. She started asking questions, like if I was planning a trip for my wife or girlfriend.

I smiled politely and halfway explained the situation, adjusting my headphones subtly, saying I wanted to be left alone. But she didn't take a hint, and she said a sentence with the last two words I ever wanted to hear:

"In memory"

I hadn't heard that yet. I'd heard "passed away," "no longer with us," "in a better place" so many times they rang hallow. Like needle pricks on a bruise. Little tingle but no real pain. But "in memory" ... In fucking memory. That was like a baseball bat to the bruise. A tooth rattling reality check that I wasn't ready for. I wasn't ready to think of her as only a memory, completely in the past tense.

I hadn't fully had that realization, and in retrospect, being trapped 30,000 feet in the air in a pressurized tube with 100 strangers might not have been the best place for it.

I admittedly snapped. I started screaming at her, telling her the shut the fuck up and mind her own business. She got so scared she, tattletales, to the flight attendant, and they asked me to move to the back of the plane so I could be "supervised." Yeah, literally got in airplane timeout.

I had to grab my stuff and walk down the aisle, getting booed and dirty looks. Mothers turning their children not to look at me. I wanted to scream at them too. I wanted to tell them to let their child stare, let them see what a broken man is. Let them see what can happen when you put your nose where it doesn't belong. Use me the way you do when you pass a car accident. Let me be an emotional seatbelt reminder. Show them a reality, give them a clear picture of how much two words can hurt someone if they are the right two.

But I figured I should just be quiet. The entire plane was already blindly against me; I didn't need to give them any more reason to be.

It was so embarrassing being escorted to the back. Having a male staff member sit in the aisle seat, trapping me to the window. I had to wait for everyone else to get off before I could even get my carry-on. I felt like a kindergartener. And the worst part was, I couldn't defend it. It didn't matter what I had to say because she was an old broad with paper-thin skin and bones that cracked like twigs; they took her side. But it wasn't fair. She attacked me. I wasn't ready for that conversation. I wasn't ready to have an illusion I didn't even know I had shattered. I was furious at the moment. But now, out of the heat of it all, I see the bitch was right.

All of this, the list, the not done living yet, it is all in her memory. I think on some level, I kept denying that. Like I convinced myself that this was a video game, and if I unlocked enough levels, it would save her. It would revive her. But it won't. She's not coming back. Ever. I can't save her any more than I could have that night.

See? "That night" carries more weight than "the night." Two letter difference completely different vibe.

Anyway, yeah guess that's the update. I have a new, most embarrassing moment; my wife is never coming back, I have no fucking idea what I am doing, and words suck. Morale of the story.

       Sincerely,
       Seat 61 K as in Kindergartener

May 26

Another box checked. Taylor Swift concert. Hey, I can't argue with the list, and honestly, it was a hell of a show.

I did something I hadn't done in a long time. I put a penny in my "good day jar." I had almost forgotten about it. Well, that's not true; I do think about it sometimes. It is my one thing in a fire. You know, like if the house was on fire and all your family and pets were safe, what is the one thing you'd grab on your way out. I'm sure you've got something like that. Maybe a sweater your grandma knit you? A photo album? An old journal? We all have that one thing.

This jar is mine. I started it when I was about 10, and every truly good day, I'd put a memento in it. And I promised that I would never remove anything. Even things from exes or now enemies. Because it wasn't a reminder of that person but a reminder of that moment. That moment standing alone, perfectly picture framed in memory. Penny found out about that box when we moved in together. She asked if she could help add things. There are all kinds of things in there. Sticks, movie ticket stubs, dried flowers, Christmas light bulbs, deflated balloons, rocks. Anything you can imagine. And pennies. Lots of pennies with painted numbers on them. Then in a small notebook in the kitchen drawer, there is a list of all the numbers and what happened on that day.

This tradition of labeled pennies took over. And every time we had a really good day, we would put a penny in the jar. And she even labeled it with glitter paint. The last penny we had put in was number 333 when she won the biggest case of her career.

That was almost two years ago. We somehow got too busy to have good days. I mean, we had some. But damn, we did not take enough time to enjoy them. We used to soak up every moment; countless dinners and picnics had silent minutes, us just looking at each other, learning each other, absorbing every drop of the moment as we could. I remember going to concerts and sports games and missing half the show because I was so enthralled with her. Thousands of screaming fans fell on my deaf ears. Flashing lights and fireworks didn't make me blink. Just she did.

But then you grow up. You build a comfortable home in the love you have. You tame the butterflies and fast forward through the slow-motion moments you always think you'll get to come back to. You settle in, and life becomes bills and grocery runs and planning a future you don't realize you are taking for granted. You treat it like it's always going to be there. It's always going to be this way.

But it won't. Someday the butterflies will lose their wings, and the slow-motion turn into agonizing empty standstills. You'll look up to the sky to see her instead of across the dining room table. You'll be screaming the lyrics of her favorite song in her memory instead of twirling her around to it. We all know this logically; we know that someday will come. But even when it's right in front of you, you are never ready for it.

So, I put penny number 334 in the jar. I never thought I would have a good day without her. But I did; it wasn't perfect. It was just a good one. And I think I need to acknowledge that.

The crazy part was, I reread some of the entries from the notebook, and I didn't feel anything. I combed back through the best moments of my life and didn't feel a flicker of emotion. No hope. No nostalgia. No overwhelming joy. No sinking pit in my stomach. Nothing. And I don't know how I feel about that. But that's okay because I couldn't feel it if I did know.

Sincerely,
Numbo, the Elephant

June 1

Well, I am not numb anymore. Guess what broke me. Go ahead, guess. Boxing up her clothes? No. Selling her car? Nah. Gum. Yep, a pack of fucking gum. I went to the store, and I had eaten a tuna salad for lunch, so my breath was awful. So, I opened my center console, and I found this pack of gum. Penny had bought it for me a few months ago. I forgot I even had it. It wasn't a big deal. It was just on-sale. It wasn't some grand romantic gesture. We aren't that couple from that one Extra commercial. The staples of our relationship were not gum.

But this is the last thing Penny ever gave me. I took the last piece and started to chew. And I stared at the empty package in my hand. Any normal human would have just thrown it away. It's trash. It's an empty paper container that has served its purpose. By every single definition, it is trash and should be disposed of. But I couldn't. I actually started to cry. A grown-ass man in the parking lot of a Kroger crying over an empty pack of gum. A Kroger that no doubt has an entire aisle of gum exactly like this one but this one was different. This was hers.

I drove away, still holding the pack in my hand. The whole drive home, I have no idea why this got to me. Like there are literally hundreds of thousands of things Penny will never do again. She will never kiss me again.

She will never steal my slippers. She will never drive that really weird way with her one leg leaning on the door. She will never say I love you again. She will never have my kids. She will never grow old with me. She will never be with me again. And those thoughts would break any normal husband but me? Nope. But the idea of her never buying discount gum again, THAT is what breaks me. Logical.

                                        Sincerely,
                                    Minty Fresh Dumbass

June 15

Yes, I know it's been a minute, I apologize, I haven't done much, I've just been down, And done, And feeling empty but yet also like there is a swirling vortex of chaos and anger and confusion inside of me, I literally feel like I'm losing it, Like losing it, Like, call me Joker fuck society losing it, I've been thinking about Annalise, Like thought thoughts, Not like, oh she looks hot today thoughts, "I love you" thoughts, Which I do, I always have, but not that way, Never that way, That has never been mentioned or on the table or even a glimmer of a thought in either of our heads,

But now, I am thinking about it, And I feel awful, In my head, I'm married, But at the same time, if there was ever going to be someone else, it would probably be Lise, I don't know, I'm freaking out, dude,

We were just having coffee catching up, and I just got this overwhelming feeling, My body even leaned in, I just wanted her, And not I've ever before, Because there have been times when instinct takes over, And I'm just like, "ooh, hot girl," But then my brain gets the blood flow and is like, no dumbass, calm down,

But this time, my brain didn't switch sides. Instead, it was like, "go for it, dumbass," And I almost did,

I mean, she looked nice. She had on a green sundress, she had just lightened her hair a few weeks ago, and it was pulled up because it was hot as hell outside. She didn't have makeup on, but her glasses magnified her eyes a bit. That is what I got caught up in. Those eyes. They knew me. They had seen thousands of variations of me. All of the real ones. If there were any two souls that knew mine, it was hers and Penny.

But the reality is a bitch. I'm married. That hasn't changed. I am dying; that hasn't changed. She still doesn't know that I am dying. That hasn't changed. Nothing has changed, but yet everything has changed. I don't know what to do. I can't avoid her; she'll know something is wrong. I can't tell her; she'll freak. And I could lose her. That is one thing I'm not willing to risk. Nope. Not a chance. Not an option. We don't even have the ingredients, let alone that being on the menu. Nope. Nope. Nope. She is all I have left, and me and my stupid heart can just stay the hell out of it. I don't need to fuck up anything more than I already have.

So yeah, there's a quick update for you; I'm losing my mind. And I'm still dying. So, yay me.

Sincerely,
Smack My Ass and Pour
Some Coco Puffs Because
I'm Fucking Coocoo

June 17

I honestly don't know what is happening or what to do. I am trying to keep a calm mindset. I am trying to use every drop of logic and reasoning I have left in me to explain the thoughts in my head, unfortunately to no avail.

Wow, that was kind of a Mr. Poetic Pants moment, "to no avail," god, who am I? I'm talking about feelings for my best friend, not a British spy who failed his mission. Yeah, so I am still having these feelings. They appear to be getting stronger. More defined even. Less blurry butterflies and clearer thought-out ideas.

I don't know how to handle it. I am trying to just convince myself that it's the meds, or it's me dying, or it's quite literally me going crazy with grief for my wife. That's the other part: if Penny was here it wouldn't be a thought in my head.

She would ask me from time to time why I never really looked at other women. I always answered with, "Why would I look at thousands of tiny stars when I'm standing inches away from my sun."

That is one of the most romantic things I ever came up with in our entire relationship. And I loved how accurately it portrayed us. Because Penny wasn't a superstar, she didn't have millions of people loving her. She wasn't on magazine covers or movie screens. She was beautiful, but that word is impossible to achieve by society's standards. She wasn't a supernova Rockstar, but she was to me. To the rest of the world, she was a flickering star, but to me, she was my sun. And the only thing that made her different was me getting close enough to her to love her. She lit up my world.

But thinking about now, there's another layer to that analogy. If I'm earth and Penny is the sun, Annalise is my moon. She was the cold one, the one who helped calm my tides, the one that got my head right. She has her own life, her own gravity, but she was always also in mine. And when I was basking in the sunlight, I never questioned the sky. Annalise was always there. She was always a shining silver, even in the brightest days. But now it's like the sun burned out, and all I have is darkness... and the moon, I can see her clearly now. Not that I couldn't before. But she's glowing, and I can't tell if it's her or just some leftover sunrays reflecting.

Okay, I took that analogy way too deep. But you see what I am saying? Am I really feeling these things, or am I just wanting to be in love again? And I really, really, really hate to ask this but I don't have a choice. What do you think I should do?

Honestly, I think you know me better than anyone. Because I don't have to lie to you. I don't have to fake it with you. That's one thing I like about you; I can just be me. And after everything, I hope that you feel the same way. Or at the very least, there is something you like about me.

Even if there isn't, I need you to put that aside and help me. Do I risk losing her? Do I ignore everything I feel? Because odds are, I'm going to be dead soon anyway. If I die without telling her, is she going to wonder? If I do tell her and she doesn't feel the same, I could die without my best friend. If I do tell her and she does feel the same, then she gets even closer, and losing me would hurt even more? Am I really in love with her? Or am I convincing myself that this illusion might be worth living for? How do I decide when all the options end with someone in pain? What the hell do I fucking do? Seriously. Nonrhetorical.

Sincerely,
King of Questions

# June 18

I had an epiphany or a mental breakdown and used unrelated things to justify something ridiculous. I'll let you decide.

Alright, so remember when you were in elementary school, and your best friend was in your class? Every time the teacher said "find a partner," you would immediately lock eyes. And because you knew each other so well, you knew how to work together. You had projects down to a science and hit every single one out of the damn park. You had a perfect A in the class and became the role model for students.

But eventually, the teacher broke you and your best friend up. Being a child, you would argue. Not understanding why you had to split when you worked so well together. And the teacher would give you some bullshit about you have to learn to work with other people.

I had that situation in 5th grade with a guy named Greg. We had a history together and were both nerdy dorks that always went one step past what was required. Eventually, Mrs. Williams broke us up and made me work with Linda Burke. She was nothing like Greg. She had no focus or attention span. She didn't want to do any of the hard work, only the fun stuff. I wasn't a fan. I very maturely asked Mrs. Williams, to switch back, and she politely told me no. I was furious. I stomped around all huffy and puffy. I rolled my eyes at everything Linda said, simply because she wasn't Greg.

I hadn't thought of that experience in years, and it randomly came to me this morning. And as an adult, I see why Mrs. Williams did what she did. Not everyone in life is going to be exactly like you. They aren't going to think or act the way you are used to, and eventually, you are going to have to learn how to deal with that. But then, my wonderful brain took it a step further.

What if God does the same thing with soulmates? What if there really is one soul you are tied to for eternity? Your bonds are unbreakable, undeniable to the point you know it even on a human level, which would explain the love at first sight phenomenon. But we are here to learn. We live this life to learn it, and just like not all people are the same, not all souls are the same, and we have to learn how to deal with them. How to love them even. It's safe to assume that the purpose of multiple lives is for us to get a complete comprehension of life. So, it's possible the same is applied to love. You can't learn everything about life in one lifetime; likewise, you can't learn everything about love by being with the same soul over and over. So, they split us up. Make us spend a life with someone else in order to learn better.

But here is the kicker: Greg was still in my class, even when we weren't together, he still was in the room, so maybe that's the way life does it too. You meet your soulmate every time, but they aren't always your life partner.

Maybe we humans have it twisted; your soulmate isn't necessarily the one you spend your life with. But instead, the one that helps you become who you are supposed to be. The one that gets you ready for the love of your life. This would explain the "one that got away" concept. I've watched people lose their soulmates. And not the way I did, I mean a breakup. And it shatters them; they can't believe it. It's like every fiber of their being blatantly denied solid facts because they just know they are their soulmate. Dangerous concept, but it's possible it's true. We hold on to our soulmates, even when they break us, even when they are wrong for the human we inhabit, even when the universe is doing everything in its power to pull them away. All because no one has told us that "love of your life" and "soulmate" aren't interchangeable. That there can be two. Sometimes it's just one, but most of the time, it's two. And that makes you stronger. Because after all, arguing with Linda that Mayan calendars didn't have glitter on them made me a better student. It made me a better person.

So maybe loving Annalise would make me a better soul. Maybe the reason I can't shake this is because I am not supposed to. Maybe this love will be what saves me. And just like Greg and I didn't stop being friends, this doesn't diminish anything I have with Penny.

Why not give it a shot? If I'm going to die, why not die loved? With a hand to hold? With everything I've got rumbling around in my head, spread out on the table? No regrets. No wonders.

I ended up getting an A on the calendar; it didn't ruin everything. Maybe this won't either. I mean, what is the worst that can happen? She says no, and we have a good laugh? We'd be fine. We all would be fine. So why suffer? Why not throw around some glitter with Linda before I get to see Greg at recess?

                                            Sincerely,
                                     My wife is a Greg

June 19

She might be a Linda. We kissed. Before you get all butterfly or fuming mad, let me explain. It wasn't some huge grand romantic moment. There was no uncontrollable outpour of emotions. It wasn't a movie scene with some noticeable tension and quiet music playing getting louder and louder into a crescendo of excitement as our lips finally meet. No, that wasn't us. That has never been our style.

We were just talking, hanging out; we went through a drive-thru and got some food. I kept looking at her; I just couldn't get my head to stop spinning. She even noticed and asked if I was okay. I wasn't sure how to answer that. I couldn't get over this idea that I had to tell her, even if it doesn't fully make sense. Even if she laughs in my face, at least there would be closure. This secret that has been twisting and turning itself around my insides would be obliterated. We haven't ever kept secrets. I don't know about you, but the thing that I value most in a friendship is honesty. You know? Like what else would it be? I judge someone based on how honest they are with me and themselves. Isn't that exactly what friendship means? Caring about someone enough, to be honest, all the time? That is my definition, at least...

It's always been a big thing of mine. That is why this was killing me so badly. Our relationship was built on a solid stack of blunt truths. But nowadays, it felt like that was all we had is secrets. Well, on my end, at least. She didn't know about my condition, my little birthday party thing, nothing.

She knew a completely different version of me, and I hated it. She has always known the real me. I knew that I had to come clean about at least some of it. Start out with the feelings, see where it goes from there. But I had no idea where to start. I mean, what do you say when you know, it's going to change everything? I knew that I had to do this right, I couldn't fuck this up because she is my best friend. And that's when it clicked; she's my best friend.

This is the only woman besides Penny I have never lied to. This is the person that knew me better than anyone. That is consistently on the same page. That has seen me at my absolute worst. Or at least what up until 6 months ago, I thought was my worst. She had stood by me in many storms and heartbreaks. We had never really fought. Never cried or screamed at each other. We handled everything rationally and logically. I realized this conversation should be no exception, so, I pulled over, and she asked me if I was okay, I answered as honestly as I could, "I don't know."

Again, talk about words having more power than they should. A sentence that has virtually no information tells the whole story.

I told her I had been having these thoughts and feelings about her lately. That I wasn't sure what to think of them or how to handle it, she got a little wide-eyed but remained calm. She didn't get flustered or angry or confused even. She just asked me to elaborate.

We sat and had a very open, honest, meaningful conversation. I asked if she had ever thought about me that way, and she said she did a long time ago, way before Penny. She convinced herself that she loved me. I was a clueless moron and didn't notice.

"But Penny didn't make me stop loving you," she said. "She just changed the filter on the love I had for you. You two were obvious. The universe made it clear you two were endgame. Destined. Meant to be. All that romantic shit I never believed in. Admittedly, at first, I was jealous, but I saw you with her. Really saw you. I saw the way you two clicked. The way your eyes lit up when she walked in the room. I saw the love she had for you before she even said it. And all that jealousy faded away. I stopped praying to be the one that made you happy and instead just prayed for your happiness. No conditions. No strings."

Amazing human. First off, holy shit. Second off, this truly surprised me. I had never thought of her feeling that way. All the times of me rambling on and on about Penny flashed through my head. All the nights Lise and I stayed up till 2 am, me gushing over how Penny could be the one. I never realized I might have been hurting her. That possibility never entered my mind. It did now, nearly a decade too late.

So once again, we were unknowingly on the same page. Curious but scared, I apologized for just dropping this on her out of the blue. She understood and agreed to talk about the idea of us.

We went back to her place, and we talked. For hours about every single thing we could think of. We expressed our fears and our hopes. We ironed out all the potential wrinkles that could come between us. We revisited our past traumas, what we won't tolerate and what we expect. Love languages. Social media presence. Me finishing the list alone. We went over every single detail to make this as transparent as possible. Except for the dying thing. I figured that is a sit-down of its own. And then ended the conversation with a pinky swear to always put our friendship first. That if at any point we jeopardize our friendship, we immediately go back to just being friends.

And then we kissed. It was planned, expected, and well-executed. It was wonderful. Felt different than anything I had ever experienced. Different than kissing Nat or any of my other exes. And somehow different than kissing Penny. Very different than kissing Penny. Her kisses always felt like laying down in a meadow. Smooth, warm grass beneath you, slight breeze, crystal clear blue skies slowly floating around you.

But this. This felt like a warm blanket. Like I was huddled up watching snowflakes fall outside a frosted window with a warm fire crackling turning the room a slightly darker orange than the gold I was used to.

It was different. Not worse or better, just different. I knew things would feel better when some of the truth was out. And I know things will feel better once all the truth is out.

    Who knows, I might not be dying. This treatment might work. They might find a cure tomorrow, and we can all clink glasses and cheers to life. I don't know; no one knows what the future holds. But I do know that at that moment, I could almost breathe.

Sincerely,
Fire Place Feelings

July 14

I was going to tell her, I swear, you heard me I was going to tell her, Everything. Every single detail down to what shirt I was wearing on my birthday and what number spot I parked in at the hospital when I got diagnosed. I was going to tell her. I was just so scared to. Things have been nice lately. So nice and cozy and loving and wonderful, and I didn't want anything to ruin that. I thought that if I keep pushing it off, it will go away. Maybe fix itself somehow. Maybe it could just blur into history, and we'd laugh about it 20 years from now. Or I would die in a few months, and then she'd find out, and it'd be like, "well, he's already dead, so I guess that doesn't matter now." Either way, a minimal amount of pain was inflected.

Well, the universe had other plans because she found her letter. Her fucking goodbye letter from me. She wasn't being a snoop; she wasn't looking for it, and she has always respected my privacy. But she has been staying over, which has been nice. She's helped take care of Lucy, she's been cooking, and we kiss and cuddle and talk; it's been amazing. But she was cleaning up the bedroom a little bit, and she found this. And as if by the hands of God himself, it fell open to her page. She saw her name, started reading, and didn't stop. She knows everything now. And I do mean everything.

I went to the store and came back to a shoe thrown in my face. She was a furious, confusing hurricane of "hold me" and "I'm gonna punch you."

She demanded answers, yelling in a way I had never heard before. I'd seen her angry before. Seen her get cut off in traffic or cheated on by a shitbag boyfriend. But this was a new level. This tone was lethal, and my name was painted on every word.

Part of me wanted to run. Run out the door off the nearest bridge. Explain things on the other side because I can't live with this. I just did the last thing I ever wanted to do: I hurt her. In her eyes, I lied. I wanted to keep things normal. But I ended up ruining everything we had, trying to save an illusion.

Let me be clear since you are now officially the only one I haven't lied to. I wasn't happy; I wasn't okay. But I felt okay. I felt like things weren't so bad. Like I was still watching the dumpster fire that is my life burn, but this time I at least had some marshmallows to roast. I wanted to ignore it, convincing myself that if I focused on the s'mores, the fire would fade into nonexistence.

But that is not how life works. And it blew up in my face. We had a long conversation, the entire time she sat arms crossed on the other end of the couch. I told her everything. Every goddamn thing. I didn't leave a single detail to her imagination. I wanted to be as open as possible. In retrospect, that's what I should have done all along.

I apologized and groveled and was practically on my knees, begging for her to forgive me. She didn't budge. She sat like a beautiful statue until she eventually said she needed to leave. Lucy ran after her and stepped in front of the door, blocking her path. I swear that dog is smarter than most humans.

It didn't work, though. Annalise still unlocked the door and walked out. I heard the door slam, and I swear I heard my heart break into pieces. She then came back in and stood in the doorway.

"You fucking tell me." Her entire demeanor had changed. Her tears had stopped; her voice wasn't yelling. She was completely calm, which made what she said sting that much more:

"You fucking tell me. You tell me when you are not okay. You tell me when the waves hit. You tell me when you are standing on the ledge because we are bros. Fuck this new whatever. We are bros first, and you need to fucking tell me."

Dagger to the fucking heart, man. I watched the door close, this time slowly. And I was left alone. Surrounded reminders of the people I've hurt. Living in a giant shrine to all the things I've fucked up. Curling up inside a cornucopia of all the loves I'd lost. I felt my chest fill with anger, feeling it pump into my veins. I wasn't mad at her; how could I be? I was angry at me. At Penny's murderer. At Penny for leaving me to figure all this bullshit out. At my lungs. At the stupid son of a bitch that I punched that got me into this mess in the first place. How nice would this have been as a surprise? Like just not waking up one day, or dropping dead in the cereal aisle at the grocery store. Yeah, scare some employees, maybe a paramedic. But that would have been better than this. The question marks are constantly floating around. The not knowing what to do or even what to think. These feelings would never have surfaced. They would just be chalked up to what could have been. A possibility in an alternate universe. But now, they are a reality.

 I guess I should have been prepared for that. I should have figured things were only going to get worse. Because no matter how much chocolate I put on the dumpster s'mores, it's still going to smell like burning trash.

      Sincerely,
      Going to Fling Myself
      into the Dumpster Fire
      That is My Life

August 8

I guess I should start with an apology. I know I have been MIA. I have been meaning to talk to you. But honestly, I have been doing really well. Pretty much everything has changed. I got a new job. This pet store opened up just down the road. It's nice, not much of a paycheck, but I get to bring Lucy to work every day. I play with puppies and kittens, and hamsters. And the customers are always happy.

Annalise and I worked things out. We had a really long talk about everything, and I promised to tell her everything from this point forward, no more secrets. It has worked for us our entire friendship. It makes sense that it would work for us now. We are still baby-stepping our way through all the milestones. But we definitely have gotten used to being around each other all the time. Things were going very well, and I was finally adjusting to this new concept of normal.

Then I went to the doctor today. He shattered my illusioned happiness quicker than even I could. My condition has worsened, which on some level, I knew I was slowly getting weaker. I got out of breath faster, even from just a simple flight of stairs. The food bags at work felt heavier. I knew it wasn't looking good.

But a stupid little part of me had faith. Some tiny few cell clusters of hope lingered in my body enough to make me think I could actually win. That me choosing to live was enough to convince life to let me. I somehow convinced myself that faith, trust, and a little positivity dust would somehow stop my lungs from deteriorating. But I guess Tinkerbell doesn't do inside jobs.

I am still dying, there is no way to deny that. Which is like, okay, I knew that. That's not breaking news; that is an idea that I have been very, very aware of for some time. But the worst part is I fucked up.

I fucked up big time; I let Annalise in. I let her see behind the "I'm okay" curtain. She went with me today. I watched her eyes widen as we pulled in; she hates hospitals always has. But here she was, for me. She listened to the doctor's every word, even taking notes on her phone. Doc was happy to see me with someone. Maybe loved people have a better chance of survival.

It was awful, I mean, hearing you are even closer to death than you were six months ago, that's one thing. But watching someone you love have to hear it and watch their heartbreak; that's worse than death itself. She held her mouth in a straight line the whole appointment. Then cried as soon as we made it to the car. She flung herself onto me and didn't want to let go.

That's when I realized what a fucking idiot I am; why the hell would I bring her into this? Because I love her? Because I got spooked? Because I have some subconscious need to destroy everything I love, so I don't have to chance to lose it? It's not fair to her, I shouldn't be able to destroy her just because I love her. I mean, in what world is loving someone consent to shatter them?

Actually, maybe that is exactly what it is... Because everyone leaves eventually. By death or by choice, we all leave. So maybe the concept of love is nothing more than someone saying being with you is worth the pain of eventually losing you.

God damn. No, No more theories right now. I need to focus on the reality of things. The actuality of things. Because that is what needs my attention.

I did this. I brought her onto this sinking ship because I was scared. I clung to her when I felt I had lost everything. I latched onto her amidst an avalanche. And now she's shivering and being pelted with snow. She's my best friend, and she's suffocating in my own snow.

So, I have made a decision. Not easily, but I made it. I can't let her love me. Not with the world ending. Not with the sky falling. I have to destroy the version of me that she knows and pray that will be enough to drive her away. If she doesn't jump ship, I'll throw her overboard. I have to make her hate me enough to leave and pray that grief is enough for her to forgive me. It sucks. It fucking sucks. And it is going to absolutely kill me to purposely hurt her. But hey, thanks to these bad boys in my chest, that will actually kill me soon anyway.

      Sincerely,
      Captain of the S.S. Avalanche

August 12th

If you could wake up tomorrow and change anything about yourself, what would it be? And I mean anything, any quality or ability that exists. Invisibility? Super strength? Power to fly? Power to duplicate money. Anything in the entire realm of existence, what would you choose?

Would I probably do something amazing like flying or super speed? How cool would that be, just like "hmm, I want Italian gelato." So, you just run across the ocean, and in like 12 minutes, you'd be in Italy. But if someone gave me that choice today, my answer would be different. I would want the ability to shamelessly do whatever I wanted.

I wish that I could be clueless and stubborn, and it has no consequences. I wish that I could just selfishly do all the things I wanted and not feel a tinge of guilt.

Because have you ever stopped and thought about the concept of being "good." Society tells us that good people win in the end. That karma is a bitch who always keeps the score even. But think of all the good people you know... How many of them have more than their share of bad things that happen? How many of them get hit harder and knocked down more than the blissful morons, you know? You know the type: clueless, self-absorbed, never cares about the bigger picture, only the pixel they live inside. And how often do THEY get hurt? Less, right? Logic.

And I know, I know we've already talked about the different levels of life and the difficulties and rewards that come with them. But I also think the way a person feels during those rewards and difficulties needs to be considered. I think the ones who carelessly do "good things" shouldn't outweigh the ones that painfully do the "wrong things" for the greater good. Or at least the good of someone else.

Case and point: tonight, I tried to break up with Annalise. I tried to do it gently. But she basically ignored me and told me to stop pushing her away. I was getting so frustrated; I was trying to help her. I was trying to save her because God knows I can't save me. I knew what I had to do.

So, I took a deep breath, looked at the reflection in the microwave door, and walked out. I knew what I had to do, but I just wasn't sure I was ready to.

I convinced myself that destroying me was the only way to save her. So, I did. I purposely forced myself to become the man I swore I wouldn't be. I channeled my inner fuckboy. I pulled forth my douchebag side. Pushing myself out of the nice guy cocoon. Ignoring my underdeveloped wings. I went to a bar, and I found a girl.

Actually, I found two, but the first one said she was with someone and pointed at this monstrous dude. He had this really cool red chain tattoo going down and all the way around his arm. If he hadn't looked so terrifying, I would have asked him about it.

While I was having a slight bro-crush moment on this dude, another girl came up. She sat down and immediately put her hand on my thigh. One look. That was all it took. No lines. No game. One kiss. Just straight went for it.

And it felt like someone kneed me in the stomach. I left so fast I expected there to be flame skid marks behind me like they have in cartoons. How I made it to the car without throwing up, I don't know. It felt like all my organs were doing straight backflips.

Oddly enough, though, I don't think it hit me this hard because of Lise. Or even Penny. Because my first thought, if I am being totally honest, was you. I thought of what you would think of me. And clearly, I have to become a different guy for her, but I don't want to be different from you. I want to be the real me with at least one person, and guess what? Lucky you.

But see, that's why I wish I could just do whatever I wanted. I wish I could not care. I wish that I could just be a mindless, selfish dickface. I wish I could break her heart without breaking a sweat. Fuck someone. Probably even enjoy the sex when I did. I wish I could easily shatter the illusion of me without a single slice on my hands. I wish that I could just walk away from burning her world to the ground without a snowflake of ash on me.

But unfortunately, mama raised me right. I am not a dick. I am a good guy. And worse off, I am a good guy that loves her. So, I had to lie.

I stayed in my car for a while, contemplating every other option. Then I came home wearing a perfume I borrowed from the drug store, I unclicked the door lock and made my way to the kitchen.

I took a moment just to remember this. Remember this feeling. Her happy, cooking in her favorite T-shirt. Her curls falling and bouncing every which way. I didn't want this moment to end, but I knew it would.

I stood there, and I went straight for it. I told her I cheated, I told her I never loved her that way, I told her that this was just some stupid rebound. That I was so grief-stricken that I went mad and fell into the delusion of believing love was an option again. I told her that this wasn't what I wanted. I lied. I lied through my fucking teeth. And then I watched her break.

I watched her eyes well up, I watched her grip on the spatula get tighter and tighter, I watched her grab a few things, apologize to Lucy and then slam the door. And yeah, that all bothered me, sure, but what really got me was the urge to fix it. I'm her best friend, I am the one who glues her pieces together, I am the one that threatens to track down the cheating boyfriend and hang him by his nuts from a powerline, I am the one who hands her the ice cream tub or the bottle of wine, I am the one that has spent the past decade fixing her. And now I am the one tearing her apart. Because I had to. Because I don't get a fucking choice.

So, in conclusion, I wish I could not care. I wish that I could live life solely for me with no consideration for anyone, even the people I love. Because if I had that ability, I would grab her and kiss her and hold her and let her love me with everything she's got. And not give a single fuck that it's going to destroy her when I leave. So that's where I am at, ether I can break her now or let my death destroy her later. I think I made the right call. Do you? I don't know. But I'll tell you this much, I don't know what death feels like, but it can't hurt worse than seeing her taillights.

Sincerely,
The Worst Good Guy Ever

August 16th

Not gonna lie, I am drunk. And alone. And freaking out. And you seem to be my go-to panic buddy so let's fucking go.

Okay. Death. Right? We, humans, have defined it. We have used words to give it physicality. But have you ever thought about it? I mean, really, really, really thought about it. Ever tried to picture death? Go ahead, take a second and picture it, I'll wait...

Nope. Wrong. You are just picturing darkness. Not non-existence. We all have our beliefs about the afterlife: reincarnation, past lives, souls. But no one knows for sure; what does it feel like? Do you even feel anything at all? Does depending on how you die depending on how it feels? Like do you have a hunch about how you will die? Like I always thought I'd die by a bullet. Ironic, I know. But seriously, even as a little kid I was always terrified of getting shot; even just riding down the road, I'd cover my head and lay in the backseat because I was convinced I was going to get shot.

I have never told anyone that before. And I know what you are thinking "how can you be terrified of guns then go and join the military?" Well, my darling when your heart gets so broken it feels like it went through a woodchipper, you go searching for anything that isn't you. Anything that doesn't remind you of your old self. And that's what I did. And I got over my fear, for the most part. And then... then... my wife got shot. How hilarious is that? How fucking Shakespearean irony right out of a damn Greek tragedy fucked up is that?

Anyway, death is a trippy ass concept. But as if the idea of ceasing to exist isn't scary enough, then you think about the fact that you do exist right now. I exist. You exist. This is life. Not a movie we are watching. Not a simulator or some Disney 3d experience. This is real. Actually. happening real shit.

We all forget that. We all walk around telling ourselves that this is our movie and everyone else is extras on set. We allow ourselves to believe we are the main characters and are somehow immortal.

"God can't kill me, I am the star of the show" that is our mindset. But in reality, God is the star of the show, and we are just the dumbfucks dressed like trees in the back.

And we wholeheartedly buy into this mindset. We say things happen for a reason or that we always get things right. No. No we fucking don't. Sometimes, we do the wrong thing. Sometimes, we do fuck things up. Sometimes things don't work out in the end. Because we make mistakes. And there are no rewinds. No pauses. No redoes. The universe has no favorites. We are all equals, no matter what life we lead. How the fuck humans managed to forget that point, I don't know. But we are all equals to the universe. And death. We are all the same size in death's eyes. It hits everyone.

But you have to wonder what does death really do? What does it take? What energy comes with you? I mean, thoughts are energy; that is a scientific fact.

And if death is an energy transfer to another existence, do the thoughts come with you? Do the memories? Is that the whole point? Make memories and lessons that attach themselves to your soul so you can reference them in your next life. Is that why we are here? And who determines what energy comes with you? God? You? Death itself? Do you take all of your thoughts with you? Like, does your soul get to carry around the backpack of depression until you shake it in your next life? Do you keep your core memories like the sad ones? The embarrassing ones? The wonderful ones? Is your soul just an old-school photo album that you slide memories in and keep for eternity? When you die, is it really peaceful? Does your body know what is happening? Does your soul know? I just don't understand it. And I hate that I don't understand it. I am a control freak. It's frustrating. And I know this is a lot to put on you, and you very well might not know the answers, and I don't expect you to. I guess I just wanted someone to wonder with. To freak out with. And apparently, you are all I've got.

          Sincerely,
          King of Questions: Death Edition

August 18th

I messed up. Big time. So, remember my little (ha little) death freak out? My drunken endeavor to the truth I wasn't ready to find? Yeah, so first off, thanks for being there, and letting me ramble, I am sure that wasn't fun to listen to. But secondly, I called Annalise. Fourteen times. I realized that in the morning, when I woke up on the kitchen floor, I did the only acceptable thing after drinking too much: I drank some more.

Eventually, she came over. And I did the absolute last thing I wanted to do: I broke. Like when was the last time you cried in front of someone? I don't mean like silent tears, politely falling, I mean loud sobbing, throwing things, collapsing on the floor feeling like legs are breaking, your heart is on a racetrack, and the oxygen in your lungs suddenly changed into molten lava. The kind of cry where shame goes out the window, and the human parts of you shatter on the hardwood.

That's what happened to me. I guess everything caught up to me, and I might not be as ready to die as I thought I was. She was cold at first, but then I watched her frosted heart melt as she knew she still loved me. Or maybe she realized she was all I had left and pitied me.

Either way, she lowered herself to the ground and wrapped her arms around me. She held herself together, very calmly and comforting, I spilled my thoughts onto her, drunk enough to ignore the stain I knew it would leave.

I told her I was scared to die. I told her I was scared to live. I don't remember much, but I knew that I wanted a pickle and broke the jar on my hand. I wanted to leave, but my jacket got stuck on the mantle. I know that I got mushy and clingy and disgusting.

I passed out and woke up on the living room floor right at sundown. My hand was covered in band-aids. My head was spinning. And my heart was fine until I saw her sitting on the couch, peacefully reading.

"Hey, how you are feeling?" she closed the book and looked at me like a lost puppy on the side of the road.

"Like shit," was the only answer my lips could form. I can't lie to her anymore. And that's when I realized. Fuck, I can't lie to her anymore.

She saw behind the curtain; she's never going to believe the show. She isn't going to fall for the tricks; she will no longer believe the mirage that I am okay. She knows, and now she is never going to let me go.

I am an idiot. She was safe. She was wrapped up and buckled in on a lifeboat, and I pulled her back on the stupid ship. Granted, no matter what, she would still have to watch the ship sink, and that would be traumatizing. But she wouldn't have to feel the boards splinter under her feet or swirl in the whirlpool as you get sucked under. She wouldn't taste the salty poison that replaces the air in your lungs as if it was the only thing allowed to exist.

I've been on this ship, I've held this ship in my arms. This ship is tattooed on me, and my name is painted on it. But just because this ship has become my home doesn't mean that I should let her move in.

I let my own stupid fears get in my head. I stopped myself from saving her. I couldn't save Penny, and now apparently, I can't save Lise.

Seems like the only person I can rescue is the one not worth saving: me. And do you know what they call a hero that only saves himself? A villain. Makes sense, actually. A broken heart is every hero's weakness and every villain's power source. Well, I've got broken hearts in spades, and let's be honest here, which one of those capes fits me better?

Damn. Another Mr. poetic pants moment, even in the shitty times that mother fucker manages to come out of me. It's just funny to me, though, because you are the only one who knows that side of me. You are the only one I can be real with.

The rest of the world sees me as this strong, smart, unbreakable real-life G. I. Joe. No poetic flowers blooming or dark clouds tale-clothing every word I say.

But you know me differently. You have watered my poetic flowers. You have felt my thunderstorms wrap around you. You have never even seen my mask the world knows me for. I have never felt the need to show it to you.

I feel calmer with you, no matter what. chaos is swirling around me. I am unafraid to be terrified with you. I am confidently weak with you. I am bluntly delicate with you, I have no reason to be or say anything other than what I want to, I may be a villain, I may be a hero, but whatever I am, I thank God, you know it best,

    That is why I feel slightly less guilty about putting you on the ship, You are strong enough to take it, You are tough enough to challenge the sea and win, The ship for you is essentially two-dimensional, I wish I could say the same for Annalise and me, But I can't, and we are stuck here, Going down together,

Sincerely,
Iceberg Ahead

September 1st

They mentioned surgery. That is the first time since the first visit that they have mentioned it. I could give you some really long boring technical reasoning but basically: my lungs are failing faster than expected.

My illness. god. "my illness." I sound like one of those kids in the commercials; everyone always changes. Let's be real; we all change it because if we don't, we feel guilty sitting there on our asses with two fully capable working legs and a relatively healthy body. We don't like having our feelings minimized. Or being reminded that someone else has it worse. That or the puppies. Dude, that shit will make the toughest man on earth cry like a little bitch.

Anyway, wow, I got off topic quickly. Can you tell I'm anxious? Basically, things are getting worse, and instead of surgery being talked about "somewhere down the road," it's very much the next exit. It went from a last resort to my only resort.

So, my choices are a very complicated, risky surgery with a long recovery, and there's a decent chance of dying on the table. Or death. Just straight out death. This is such bullshit. It was like I've arrived at the cafe of demise, and God is my waiter, and his opening line is "Hi, welcome to the end. Would you like Death or Death Lite?"

And I'm going to be completely honest; I am not sure which I want, if any at all. I know that for the past nine months, you have heard me go on and on about how I can't wait for death, I just wish I was dead, Life isn't worth living. But of course, right as I stop feeling that way, it knocks on my door.

    I am unbelievably torn on it. On the one hand, I could refuse it, I could go home and curl up with Lucy spend a few months full of pain and misery, I could let my skin turn grey and all my hair fall out, I could let the muscles fall off my body and allow my self-pity to swallow me into a gaping hole of depression, I could let my last breaths be jagged and blood-covered, I could ruin the comforter, I could let the real version of me shrivel and die into a sad, wrinkled shell of a man that was too scared to fight for his life. That doesn't sound like the best choice, but it has it's perks. No needles poking me, My flesh remains intact, untorn, and stitched. I could say goodbyes. Actually, say them instead of writing them out. Die the way God intended. That's Death.

    On one hand, it could be a success. I could be completely fixed, and either live a long, happy life or at least long enough to get on the transplant list. Then be as good as new. I could go for runs and swim in the ocean and laugh and dance and be better than I ever imagined I could be. But I feel like this hand of chance has a filter on it. I feel like what I am picturing is not my lungs getting fixed but my heart. And I am not sure that would be the case.

    On then, somehow, there is another hand: this surgery could fail. They could nick an artery, or my lungs could collapse. It could be a sweet death instead of a painful one, I'd be under anesthesia, floating carelessly in my subconscious. I probably wouldn't even know I was gone until I saw Penny. It could be an easy way out. A simple conclusion to an unraveled story. No one would see it. Annalise wouldn't get to see me or touch me. She wouldn't have to hold my lifeless hand as the paramedics pulled me away. It would be easier for her too. Receive the news in a pleasant waiting room, not the chaos of ambulance lights and sirens.

Don't get me wrong; I am terrified of dying at the moment. Simply because of the unknown. But part of me thinks it might be nice to never grow old. It might be nice to die with the body of a 35-year-old, and even more so the mind of one. It might be nice not to have my brain deteriorate. To not forget things or have society treat me like a child. It could be peaceful to go with a solid mind. It could be heroic to die with such viable organs; I could save someone else. I could do some good. Imagine how wonderful it would be to be at the end of your life and still have your 30-year-old brain? Or body... Which would you want? If you had to let one age and decay and could keep one forever, which would you do? Tough choice. I have the possibility to keep both till the very end. I could die in a breath of grace, with a sound mind and a healing body. And as scared as I am of what is on the other side of that bright light, I almost like the idea of that.

I am not wishing for it; I am making peace with any possible outcome. That way, no matter what happens, I am prepared. As prepared as you can be, I suppose. I am praying for a sign on what to do, I am hoping that somehow the sky spells it out for me, That Penny makes a visit and shines the light I have always known to be hers on the situation, I hope that she'll reach down and guide me, I hope she hasn't forgotten me, Praying that she will help me make at least one more good decision in my life, Because when the night falls, and the choices are all starting to look good, I don't know who else to turn to,

                        Sincerely,
                        Leaning Towards Death Life

September 9th

You won't believe this shit.
So, I have really been struggling with this whole death or death lite thing. I've been wondering if my life is even worth fighting for at this point. Needless to say, my brain has been running at a set pace of a thousand miles an hour. And to make matters worse, tomorrow is the one-year anniversary of Penny... dying. Annalise has been treating me with kid gloves all week. Just being overly nice, helpful, and compassionate.

I decided it was time to go and try to see the grave again. I haven't been back since the time they wouldn't let me in. I didn't feel a need to. In my mind, she wasn't there. Ya know? I felt her in experiences, I felt her in places she had been to once; I felt her joy lingering around thru the air ducts, I felt her in the home we had built together. She had never been to the cemetery she laid in.

It's a weird concept when you think about it. But we humans find comfort in widely accepted illusions. Like our loved one's souls are where we put their bodies. Or New Years' is a reset button. That firework-shaped weeds can make wishes come true. Or some numbers are luckier than others. We have established these warm snuggly lies that we find ourselves not only believing but passing down like fairytales.

And in our darkest moments, we cling to them like security blankets. No matter our age, we hear our mother's wives' tales and our father's wisdom poking through. We start rationalizing fate, flipping coins, and using flashing traffic lights to make our decisions. But sometimes they can be good things. The placebo effect is a scientific phenomenon; if you believe something is working, it will work with obvious exceptions.

I went to the grave, and I decided to allow myself into the illusion she was there. And I had to convince myself this, the whole drive. And then I got to the gate and dragged my feet down to the second to the last row. I kept my head down, trying to prepare myself to see the stone when it wasn't new and shiny. But I looked up, and all I see are sunflowers, DOZENS of them. Just randomly planted around. I could tell they were newer and definitely planted, not natural. It broke me. I cried and spilled my heart all over the ground. I'll keep exactly what I said between us, but it was quite cathartic. I didn't realize how much I was holding on to. I went through all 5 stages of grief in the course of 30 minutes. But eventually, I just ended it with; I wish you were here to help me. And left.

But here's the crazy part, on the way out, I ran into a maintenance guy. Out of curiosity, I asked where the sunflowers came from. He told me that they don't know, but it is being considered an act of "vandalism," and they were scheduled to be removed in the next two days. We got into a conversation, and I told him they were Penny's favorite and is there any way I could keep them. And he said... he fucking said: "Oh yeah, I can give you a number to call and you can tell them you're the account holder,

You might have to fight a little bit, but it will be worth it."

YOU MIGHT HAVE TO FIGHT A LITTLE BIT, BUT IT WILL BE WORTH IT

Are you kidding me? My baby showed up, I asked her for a sign, and she basically took over this man's body and used his words to speak. She hasn't forgotten me. And she wants me to fight to live, and damn it, that's what I am going to do. No more looking at clocks and red lights; I know what I need to do. I am going to start researching this surgery, how to prepare for it, how to recover from it. Everything I need to know to beat this stupid thing. I'm going all in the pedal to the medal, 110%. I am ready to live; I am ready to be okay. Even if that is miles down a very hard road, it's worth fighting for.

Sincerely,
Finally Got My Sign

September 10th

One year. Fuck.

September 14th

There is never one moment. So, stop fucking waiting for it.

Hi, good morning. I saw something on tv, and it pissed me off, so I'm going to rant about it.

It's bullshit. Every success story you hear they always tell you of "their moment." The turning point that led them to the end goal. Which sure, they may have had a moment where they realized something for the first time. But what they don't tell you is the billions of moments after that one. The ones filled with fear and doubt. The moments they lost faith and almost quit. They lost purpose. And they had to choose it over and over and over again.

Life is like love; nothing is automatic. It's a choice. Everything is a choice. It is a choice to chase down your dreams. It's a choice to give up on them. But if you think for one second that you only have to make that choice once, you're out of your goddamn mind. You make it every day. Every moment of every single day.

Success, no matter what your definition might be of it, is only achieved with love for yourself. I know that makes me sound like a self-help book but seriously. Think about being in love with someone. Enthralled with someone. The kind of love where you would go to the ends of the earth just to see them. The kind you would drive three hours and spend 2 weeks planning their birthday present. The kind where their needs and happiness are put above everything in your life except God and breathing.

Now, imagine if you did that for you. What a fucking concept, huh? Loving yourself into the life you've wanted to live. Settling for nothing less than your highest expectations. Only letting people who support that vision have access to you. Because at the end of the day, it's you, dude. You are the only one that has the power to consent to changes in your life. You are the one that controls how it goes, how things evolve, how they fit together.

So, yes, have the "moments." Breakup with the toxic partner. Cut your hair. Move halfway across the country. Pull a Penny move and let a coin decide your fate. Call it your defining moment. You're rebirth. But understand it won't be your only one. It will just be the one that someday makes the highlight reel.

While I was stewing on this concept, I had a realization of what my true purpose was. And I honestly didn't have an answer. I didn't know what I was supposed to be doing. But then I realized it was the thing I loved most. The only damn thing I've ever been good at: loving Penny. Lucy showing me that list was my "moment." And finishing it is the true purpose of my life. What's left of it, at least.

This isn't a new purpose, just a new version of it. I have to show my love in a different way now. And I need to focus up. All these tangents: Nat, Annalise, treatments. They were all distractions. I lost focus. I have to choose it again. I have to. There are only a few things left on The List. I don't care how sick I get, I don't care if my lungs give out or burst or bleed or fill up with banana pudding.

Me not pulling that trigger was my rebirth. I am back and seeing things clearer than ever. I know what I have to do. And who knows, if I live past this, then I'll find something new. But finishing my wife's legacy is what I need to do.

That's why I am telling you. Stop wasting your life waiting for "defining moments." Make your own. Quit the job that makes you want to jump out a window. Kiss the one you can't stop thinking about. Go to the gym when you have no idea what you are doing. Write the book. Draw the thing. Love her. Love him. Forgive the ones that have hurt you, not because they deserve it but because you deserve peace.

Whatever it is, seriously, whatever the fuck it is that makes your life better, choose it. Chase it. You want a moment? You want a sign. Here it is. This is it. Me telling you to choose it. Thank me for your acceptance speech.

I know I am coming in hot, but I just don't want you to end up like me. Figuring all this out at the end of your life instead of the middle. I want to give you a chance to change your ending.

Seriously, this hotheaded angry rant comes from a place of love. But choose it, never stop choosing it. Ever. You'll mess up. You'll get knocked down. Life will throw curveballs and things you never saw coming. But remember, it's part of the lessons, and what you learn

from those fuck ups will help you be better in the end.
Just don't lose focus.

Now let me be clear, don't focus so much on one thing you miss the rest of your life. Enjoy the moments not related to your dreams. The champagne giggles with your friends, the porch conversations with your mom. The little things, don't miss those. Just choose happiness. Over and over and over. Even when you feel like the sky is falling and the earth is cracking beneath your feet, look for happiness. It's there. It may be a tiny firefly, but it's there. And never stop choosing to see it. I know this rant is all over the place, but it's just coming to me, and it seems so important that I needed to tell someone.

Sincerely,
Thanks or I'm Sorry
Whichever Fits

September 30

"Perfect"

It's an intriguing and daunting word. A seemingly unattainable concept, but rarely, it glimpses by a lucky few. Add the word perfect to the long list of things humans have messed up. We toss words like that around like confetti, excitement for a moment, and then discarded and forgotten on the floor. Everything from a dinner reservation time to an asymmetrical smear of cream cheese on a bagel, we say, is perfect. But very few things actually are.

What would be a "perfect day" for you? I mean truly, no problems, no flaws, every single thing from the song on the radio to the color of the traffic light going exactly the way you want it to. What would that be for you? It's hard to imagine, right? Normally there is one wrong thing that jinxes the steak. But as crazy as it sounds, today I had a perfect day.

Annalise and I flew to Amsterdam; one of the things on the list was the Van Gogh Museum. Being a painter who loved the sky and adored sunflowers, Van Gogh was Penny's favorite artist. She always dreamed of making it to his museum. We had always planned on going, but there was always some excuse: not enough money, not enough time, no one to watch Lucy. But this time around, I throw all cares out the airplane window. I didn't care how much it cost, I didn't care how much time I had left, I found a dog sitter, I packed my shit, and I went.

Only here for 3 days, quick trip because all I really care about is checking the box. I am sure there are many beautiful sights and fun nightlife activities. But I didn't care; I know what I came to do.

So, my perfect day started by waking up to the sunrise turning our all-white hotel room a beautiful golden orange. Then I drank some delicious coffee. Then took a perfect temperature shower. Then we went to the museum.

It was this huge, glass building, and there was a giant sunflower maze at the entrance. It was breathtaking. Just thousands and thousands and thousands of these bright, happy petals shining everywhere. It was fascinating how just a tall, lanky flower made a place I've never been to feel like home.

We did the walkthrough tour. We read about the history; we saw some of his famous paintings. I learned quite a bit, actually. But my favorite part of it was when Annalise went to the gift shop, I excused myself to the bathroom but made my way back down a hallway we had passed earlier.

I did a subtle sweep for security, and then I found a bench, tucked in the corner, pushed up against the wall, with a replica of one of Gogh's many sunflower pieces framed above it. I determined this was the perfect spot.

I had brought one of Penny's (hundreds of) sunflower paintings with me. I had it laminated and managed to sneak in a roll of packing tape in my jacket pocket. I taped her painting up underneath the bench, along with a small sign that read:

"Legacy in Sunlight"

Artist: Penny L Bailer

The wall was dark and shadowy; surely only toddlers who are too young to speak would ever notice it.

I didn't want to risk it being noticed or taken down, so I figured this was the safest place to put it. Her work was worthy of being in museums. It was worthy of being painted into murals. It should have gone viral and trended with people ripping her off by putting it on T-shirts and coffee mugs because it was for the "aesthetic." It was so fresh and beautiful and expressive. She painted feelings into a 2D form. She had pictures that felt like the comfort of a warm breeze. And others that made your head swirl. She was gifted in many things, but painting and love, we, by far her best two. She deserved to be known, she deserved a legacy, and if I can't give her that, the least I can do is give her a spot next to her idol.

This put me in the best mood I've had in a while. To be able to do something for her, I couldn't even tell anyone, but it made me the closest I've been to happy in an entire year.

It made me realize legacies are inevitable. And we essentially have no control over them because, at the end of the day, people only remember us for how we made them feel. The emotions we give people will always outweigh the time or money we shared with them.

Van Gogh is only legendary because people loved his work. Because he invoked something within them, it had almost nothing to do with him as a person. Makes you wonder why as a society, we put so much pressure on the idea of a legacy when we actually have no control over it at all.

Then I think maybe not everyone gets one. Maybe some of us, like me, are meant to be the clapping crowd instead of the Rockstar on stage. Maybe some of us are just meant to be love interests or sidekicks in the big picture. But we aren't any less important. Just because there might not be a mark on the world when we leave doesn't mean we weren't here. We were. We lived, we laughed, we loved. We stood from the sidelines, cheering on our superstars as they launched to the clouds. Or we huddled down and built our own world instead of interfering with the real one. We aren't any less important, just because there are no statues in our honor or no holidays on our birthday. I think some of us need to be happy on the ground; otherwise, reaching the stars wouldn't be so spectacular.

So definitely a thought-provoking trip. We still have one day left, not sure what we will do, but I'm sure I will let you know. But I just wanted to tell you about my perfect day. Because I never thought I would have one of those again. I know that I am pretty negative when talking to you, that we are more bitching buddies than besties, but I guess I just wanted to tell you, it's not all bad.

Sincerely,
Okay with Being
Legacy-Less

November 5th

I did it. I crossed every single thing on the list off. The last thing that I have been honestly putting off: skydiving. Ha-ha yep, I married one crazy bitch. But I did it. Either she or I did every single thing.

It took some negotiation with a friend of a friend. I mean, what moron would let a dude with chronic respiratory issues jump out of an airplane? Lucky for me, that moron exists. It took some convincing, but I didn't have to lie at all. I told him the truth. I told him I'm scared of the surgery; I'm scared of death. But that I had to go into that OR with my love's list completed. Just in case.

I mean, that is logical, right? Better safe than sorry. I mean, shit, could you imagine if I didn't, and I died? One tiny box taunting me with no way to be resolved. That would be like OCD hell for eternity.

So, I did it. Annalise came with me; I think more for her sake than mine. I could tell this made her nervous. Her leg was bouncing, and she pulled at the skin on her lip the entire safety brief. I was 99% sure she was going to cry as soon as my plane took off.

I, on the other hand, wasn't as nervous. I wasn't nervous for me at all; I was nervous for Annalise. I was anxious for the guy I would be tied to. But I didn't feel a butterfly flutter for my own safety.

Being up in that tiny plane felt like a different world. The guy opened the door, and somehow the world went silent for me. I didn't hear wind shooting by us as god-knows-what mile per hour. The hum of the engine faded. I looked up first and saw the sky, crystal clear and the bluest I'd ever seen. Then I looked down and saw clouds. They looked so bouncy, like I could just hop right on them and start skipping.

Then we jumped. Total freefall. I thought back to all the airplane windows I had looked out of the past few months. I closed my eyes, and I felt something I hadn't felt in years: peace.

True, honest, calming, silent yet deafening peace. A second where I felt every good moment I'd ever known all at once. Thousands of extinct hugs and smiles flashed before me, a wave of tranquility crests on my racing heart, slowing it down. It was a completely different high than I was expecting.

He pulled the shoot, and we floated for what felt like hours. Eventually, sashaying to the ground. I'm not going to lie to you. That ride changed me. I feel different. The air feels different. The ground feels different. It's almost like seeing life from a different perspective changed it.

Annalise jumped on me, not even trying to hide the sense of relief she had. We went back to her car, and I began to ramble about the experience.

Then seemingly out of nowhere, a huge thunderstorm came rolling in. The rain pounded the windshield in sheets, and the thunder boomed what felt like our roof.

"Penny is saying, good job," Annalise laughed. It made me smile to her mention Penny. She pulled the car off on the side of the road, and I realized we were at the cemetery. I was so caught up in my story I didn't even notice we weren't heading home.

"I was going to bring you here anyway before she quite literally stole my thunder," She joked, gesturing about.

I stayed silent for a moment, not sure what to think.

"Oh, come on," she laughed, "Thunderstorms were practically Penny's trademark. Go, go tell her all about it, and I'll be here when you are ready."

Incredible. Can you believe that? She really did respect my marriage. Despite her own feelings and wants, she loves me enough to put what I need first. I cannot believe that I have managed to find two women in my life that are this fucking incredible.

I kissed her cheek and thanked her without saying a word. I got out and made the walk that I thought I would hate. Most of the sunflowers had either died or been removed; everything was dark and cold and wet and dead.

I sat down crisscross applesauce, and I told her everything. I let the words I had spent months dreaming of saying roll off my tongue, slow enough to savor the feeling of them.

"We did it, baby."

Again, I'd like to keep exactly what was said between her and me. But I'll tell you this; I poured my heart onto that granite. I laid it all out unapologetically. And

I've mentioned this before, but Penny was always the "spiritual" one. She had always been more connected to greater things than me. I was more rooted in my brain and logic, I suppose.

But in this moment, I found myself asking for a visit. Not a sign. Not answers. No questions. Just a hello. I am still skeptical, but in that moment, I would have given anything to see a ghost and shit my pants... Well, ghost Penny, anyone else would just be awkward and terrifying.

Like, oh hi, Mr. Dead Person Guy, I understand you just broke out of the afterlife dimension and made it back into the physical world, and that's great, but you're not the one I wanted sooo could you, like, go back?

Awkward. But I kept looking around for anything, anything that could be a visit. I looked for a bird, I looked for a standing sunflower, I looked for branches shaped in any letter I could recognize. Nothing.

I was just about to give up hope when I decided to close my eyes. Almost instantly, I felt the freefalling feeling again. My senses became hyperactive. I heard each click and clack of the raindrops hitting headstones. I felt individual chills roll down my neck and onto my arms. I could faintly smell the dying petals. I practically saw the dead grass and the buildings that looked like Legos. The constant buzz in my ear stopped. The snake that had spent the past year coiled around my lungs, he disintegrated. I felt pressure on my shoulders and the center of the top of my head. Not pain, just warm, steady pressure, and immediately an image flashed in my mind.

Clear as day; it was of the picture my sister had taken of Penny and me at the beach. We were talking about something. It was a long time ago, one of the first family trips Penny got to go on with us. She was sitting in a lawn chair, and I sat between her legs. She put her arms on my shoulder and rested her chin on my head. My sister thought it was sweet, so she snapped the picture. It was candid but had arguably our best smiles. I wasn't sure why I was suddenly seeing this, but then it hit me.

In this moment, I felt the same physical pressure I did in that picture. She hugged me, my love hugged me. I am not even going to try to act tough on this one. I wept. I openly fell over and cried. I never thought I would feel her again. We were right "till death do us part" is for quitters. She showed up. Once again, she showed up when I needed her to.

I left the grave with a smile cemented to my face, still wearing the freefalling feeling like a comfy old T-shirt. I expected it to go away, to fade with the rainclouds, but it has been a full day, and I still feel it. I feel the peace. I have no fear or anxiety. I honestly don't know if that is a good thing or not, but I am okay. I don't know what to think of it or how to handle it, or how long it will last. But I am milking it for every second I've got. I wish I could capture this feeling, I wish I could bottle it up. Send it to everyone I know. Start giving it away for free. God, I would walk around town with a jar of it, throwing it in people's faces, dancing like a happy leprechaun. I wish I could share this feeling with you, I wish it was transferrable. I wish I could somehow pound it into these words and hope it somehow gets envelops you the way it has me. But it doesn't work that way, sadly. But God damn, I wish it did.

                                                                      Sincerely,
                                                                     Got a Little
                                                                     Piece of Peace

November 5th

Hey, I know I have been MIA lately, and I'm sorry. I just have been doing really well. Mentally at least. Physically, not so much; let's start with that.

To put it in normal people's terms: I am not doing well. The doctor says I need to build up the strength in the rest of my body in order for me to get the surgery. If I am too weak, they can't operate. How about that Shakespearian bullshit? I need to not be dying in order for them to save my life. And the craziest part is if this surgery works, and that is a big IF, it doesn't save me; it buys me time. More borrowed time that I am honestly unsure if I want anymore. Don't get me wrong; I do not wish to die; I just want a quality of life. I don't want to spend my last days with machines doing the things my body can't. I don't want to sit up at night praying that someone dies and I can get their lungs. I don't like the idea of trading one life for another. If it could work like that, I would have traded mine for Penny's in a heartbeat. I am not sure that I want to fight; I am not sure I want to die. I am stuck in this weird limbo, but the crazy thing is, I'm happy. I am happy here. Do I like coughing what feels like razor blades into my throat? No. Do I like getting winded from a walk down to the mailbox? No. But do I have a level of peace I haven't felt in years to the point where I am so secure in my existence, I am okay if it ends here? Yes.

If the end of my life is near, I'd want this feeling to be my last one. If it's not, and I've got another 20 years left, fucking awesome. But if it is, I want to go out feeling this much peace.

And pride. My god. I don't think I have ever been this proud of anything in my life. Finishing her list gave me a new sense of confidence, a boost of energy that has lasted months now. I used to not want to talk about her passing because it was so painful, but I have done the impossible. I have found joy and something positive in something I quite literally thought would kill me. I tell everyone now because the story has such a better undertone. It's like this, imagine your greatest accomplishment. When you won that game, when you got that girl, when you landed that dream job, picture the exact moment you did. You know that feeling? The one you got as they put the medal around your neck. The one you got when you heard someone you didn't know singing your song. The one that was hung on the walls of your brand-new corner office. That "I did it, and nothing else in all of the existence matters" feeling. Try living in that nonstop for two months, and that's where I am at. I still feel the peace I did in the cemetery in the rain. It's amazing; actually, I can close my eyes, and I feel like I am back there. I can almost hear the rain splashing, I can faintly smell the dying sunflowers and feel the warmth on my shoulders. It is like my brain has set a new default setting.

My mind has been going on all kinds of expeditions as well. Small moments of either total clarity or temporary insanity; still to be determined... I have some more very intriguing and interesting ideas. At least they are interesting to me, so naturally, you get to hear all about them.

But another time, I guess, because I have a certain golden retriever that is laying on my lap and nudging the pen out of my hand. She's been much more clingy nowadays; hasn't left my side. So, I guess I need to go give her some love. I'll talk to you soon, though, I promise.

Sincerely,
Human Pillow

November 28th

I went to the doctor today, and he gave me a few things to help me get strong enough to have the surgery. A couple of exercises I need to do, one new pill to add to the rainbow collection I already take, and of course, an unneeded amount of positivity and hope. Before you start calling me a bitter old Scrooge, I am not saying positivity isn't a good thing. I am not saying that it isn't a well-rounded, helpful tool that can help you through certain situations. What I am saying is too much of it can be a toxic mindset. It just rubbed me the wrong way to the point I thought about it the whole drive home. So naturally, I wanted to go off on someone about it. Annalise is already having a hard time holding herself together; I can tell this is scaring her way more than it's scaring me. My mom and dad wouldn't understand; they are practically the mayors of positivityville. So that leaves you.

Alright, here's the truth. Are you ready for it? You are going to have bad days. Bad things are going to happen. No matter how centered your chakras are. No matter how much hope you've got flooding your veins. Sometimes life just sucks because it does. Sometimes the world is awful. Sometimes people lie. Things fall apart. The sky starts falling. The earth splits between your shoes. Your car breaks. Your heart breaks. You get up from one hit, and life comes banging with another. Sometimes it gets loud and painful and terrifying. But you know what? You are allowed to feel that pain. You are allowed not to be okay. You are allowed to be scared out of your goddamn mind. You're allowed to scream at the falling clouds and break bottles on the cracking earth. Just don't be the one that empties them.

This whole idea of "just be grateful" or "it could be worse" or "just be positive" is crap. Those statements are valid and great ideas, but it's part of the process, not the entire process itself.

Think of it this way. If you are trying to paint an entire room yellow and you spill a can of black paint on the floor, what do you do? You don't just ignore it. You don't just continue to shuffle around like everything's normal; you'd have black footprints everywhere. You acknowledge it. You find a healthy outlet, and you soak it up. You face it head-on. You handle it at the pace you feel comfortable at, and you do your best to not let it stain the hands you need to pray with.

Depending on how deep it goes, you sand the floor down, removing the parts of your life the issue was attached to. You look around and try to figure out why there was black paint in here in the first place. If possible, you get rid of the can; if not, you move it to a corner where at least you know where it is. You take precautions so that it doesn't spill again. All the while knowing life always has the final say in the splatter.

But my point is you feel it; you go through it. You accept it for what it is and give it your all to fix it. You accept that there will be some stains that don't come out, and that is okay. It doesn't make your house any less beautiful. It shows you've lived. It shows what you have survived. The black stains will make the yellow feel even brighter. Then once the majority of the black paint is cleaned up, THEN you crack open the yellow paint. Then you bust out the one in a million, and the meant-to-be's. But I feel like everyone just skips to that part. Like it is suddenly not okay to struggle. It is suddenly not okay to allow yourself to feel the entirety of what you've been given. Instead of just shoving it down, ignoring it, covering it with a "you'll be fine" band-aid.

But we've got it wrong. We have to deal with the black paint first. Think about it, if you just took that yellow paint can and poured it into the puddles of black, what happens? You lose it all. You lose the yellow, you lose the black. And life becomes one huge, gloopy, sticky gray mess. And having a few black spots in your house is one thing, but who wants to live in a house that feels like you stepped into a monotone filter? You have to deal with the painful truths of life in order to understand the joys of it.

Now I am not saying that I am hopeful for this surgery; I am not saying that I don't pray to God every night that I live through it. I am just saying I am taking it for what it is, and I don't think that is a bad way to look at things.

Sincerely,
Your Favorite Rant Buddy

December 2nd

So, it's 2 a.m. and I was dreaming about something, and I jolted upright thinking about you. I recognize this is going to seem really random but bear with me, I just need to get this out.

I just realized that I have consistently been talking about God and souls and the universe and all these things I believe in, and I never even stopped to consider that you might not.

I am truly sorry; I get so caught up in my life I forget my point of view isn't the only one to exist. So, I apologize if anything I have expressed to you has offended you in any way. I hope it hasn't. I hope that you were just like, "yeah, sure agree to disagree, bro." I respect any kind of belief except for ones rooted in evil. So, I don't want you to think that if you do differ from me, I am damning you to hell.

I don't think it works that way anyway. I just can't imagine the concept of millions of souls burning for eternity for having different faiths. It just doesn't sit right with me. And naturally, I started thinking about how things might work.

Here is the analogy I have come up with (don't you love my analogies). Okay, life is schooling; we've established that already. Well, do you remember in middle school history when you'd get to the Civil War, and the teacher divided the room in half. Half of us were on the North, and half of us were on the South, and we had to present projects and shit.

Obviously, not a single person on the Southern side thought that slavery was a good thing, but for the sake of our grade, we had to research and convince ourselves to temporarily believe in it.

I think that religion is like that too. Deep down, we all have faith in what is true. But in order for all of us to learn better, souls take on human forms that back different beliefs.

This both shows differences in perspective and also gives us a new respect for our own. This idea also explains why we are all different, look different, sound different, have different abilities. Because again, no one would ever learn anything if we were all the same.

Anyway, I just needed to get that out. People are different because that's what we are supposed to fucking be. And I am sorry if anything related to my beliefs, well actually, anything I've said at all has offended you. But with you is the only place I can be authentically honest, and I am not going to change that. So, I am going to continue to ramble even when it's rooted in belief or faith or insanity because I need to. There is no telling what is down the road for me, so this is the time to get it all out.

Sincerely,
Thank you for coming to
My 2 a.m. TED Talk

December 5th

Knock, knock... another realization... another realization who I don't have anyone else to tell, so buckle up this is a biggie.

First off, I'll tell you that I have stayed in the same condition as last time we talked. Not getting any worse, but not any better. But as of this moment, I am on track to get my surgery. Wait, no, the surgery. I don't like calling it mine. Like not owning it makes it any less terrifying. It doesn't. I'm honestly not even that scared. I am okay with whatever happens. At least I think I am. But the concept of death is still scary as fuck. Reaching the end of the line. The drip finally stopping. Wondering in your last moments if you did what you were meant to or if your life has been a consistent stream of wrong decisions.

Boom. Perfect Segway to my realization. Purpose. Life's purpose specifically. So, let's start by diving into the basics, the old reliable of bullshit we say when things we don't want to happen:

"Everything happens for a reason."

Everything from a death to a red light, we use this worn-out line as a security blanket. We hear that hundreds of times in our life. Over and over and over until we find ourselves believing it, that is the one thing that everyone tells you.

But here is what they don't tell you:

1. The reason isn't always for you

2. You don't always get to know the reason

I know it sounds crazy but roll with me. But let's take a journey down the Hypothetical Lane. Let's say you fuck up. You miss the train and are late to work for the like 4th time in a week. You walk in, and the boss immediately fires you. Frustrated, you go to a coffee shop and meet a girl named Julie. You hit it off and end up dating.

Now pause; at this moment, everything makes sense for you. You believe that you and Julie are meant to be and are thankful for losing your job because she only works midday shifts, and you would have never met her if you hadn't been fired. You are standing there thinking you know exactly why everything happened the way it did. And because of this and you being in love, you believe that Julie is the love of your life.

Except she's not. And y'all break up. You're heartbroken. She's going through some stuff and decides to go visit her older sister. In the woes of heartbreak, they both try some hard drugs. Julie is fine. But her sister becomes an addict.

Years go by, and amongst many of the bad decisions in her life, Julie's sister gets pregnant by some deadbeat. Their kid, let's call him Peter, grows up in a toxic environment, develops all kinds of social and emotional issues, and is an addict by the time he is in his teens.

But at 18, our boy Peter has a wake-up call. His friend ODs. Seeing his lifeless body and a glimpse at Peter's possible future is enough to set him straight. He struggles for many years bouncing between being clean and not. He gets a shitty retail job; he meets a girl and falls in love.

They work their asses off, break their way into the middle class and eventually have a baby of their own. When that kid is 8, his uncle dies of cancer. This shakes the child to his core, and he begins to gain interest in the medical field. He goes through 28 years of schooling then spends another 12 years doing research and testing. Then at age 48, he finds the cure to cancer.

Happy ending, right? Feel-good story. But here is the crazy part, if one of those things had gone differently, the end result could have been changed. Think about all of the pain and suffering that got us to that point. You and Julie were hurt. Her sister and baby daddy had a rough life. Peter's friend literally died. Not to mention the people we didn't mention. Julie's mom, who watched both of her daughters' struggles. Peter's friend's girlfriend having to put her soulmate in the ground. Hundreds of people had to endure varying levels of pain in order for us to arrive at the amazing discovery.

But here is the even crazier part. None of them know that they are a part of it. You don't even know. Because it has been a good 60-70 years since you and Julie broke up, you'll be sitting in the nursing home holding the hand of your wife of 40 years. Hugging and crying as the newsflash comes in. All the while having no idea that you being a dumbfuck and missing a train is one of the reasons it happened. You'd have no clue.

So, the amazing part is you are a part of a picture so large you will never know what you give to it. But the scary part is you never know what your purpose is. Your purpose could solely have been to break up with Julie.

Isn't that a mind-blowing thought? That your entire existence could only really have one moment that is essential on a grander scale? Everything in your life could be a bonus except one cup of coffee or one red light, which honestly, there are two ways to look at that.

Either one, you say, well, if only one moment of my life matters, what is the point of living the others? Or you can look at it as only one moment matters, but we never know which one, so I've got to make all of them count.

You never know when it's your turn to drop a tile in the mosaic, which means you don't know if you've done it yet.

How awful would it be if you gave up before you did? You get to the afterlife, and God shows you what could have been. Shows you how you could have saved the world without even knowing it. Displays a universe that is proven to be incomplete without you.

Did you hear that? The universe, the single most complex, incredible, amazing thing in all of existence, is incomplete without you. It needs you until you fulfill your purpose, whatever that may be. You may not know what it is, but you have one, I promise you. I like to think mine is living for Penny, but I truly don't know. But I know that I have one; I know you have one. We might even have the same one; who knows. But I do know that we wouldn't be here if we didn't, and that thought alone is enough to live for.

                    Sincerely,
                    Not Purposeless After All

December 13th

I feel like the only thing I even talk to you about anymore is these crazy ideas I have buzzing around in my head. I am feeling as though I am dissolving into a mess of epiphanies and question marks. Both terrifying and exhilarating simultaneously. But I don't want our relationship to feel like a class or a stream of presentations. So, I will start by telling you five random things going on in my life right now, I'll wade you into the deep stuff that I usually just cannonball into.

1. My favorite blue sweater died this morning. I put it on, and the underarm of the sleeve ripped, which is weird because I have literally never been skinnier. I loved that sweater. It was one of those classy without trying looks. And it was decently warm, which was nice; it felt like more layers than it was.
2. I was messing with some planks in the garage and got a splinter in my left thumb. It is driving me absolutely bonkers. It Doesn't hurt, just annoying.
3. Annalise found a new Chinese restaurant that delivers to the house. It has the best egg rolls I've ever had. I haven't been eating a ton lately, but I ate like 12 of those motherfuckers.
4. Lucy has been stockpiling socks for god knows how long. I moved the tote her food is kept in, and no joke, 30 socks fell out from behind it. All kinds of

socks, mine, Penny's, Annalise's, a baby sock I'm not sure who it's even from. Apparently, I have raised a thief. I had to laugh though, all of us had noticed socks missing but never enough to look for them. Then the cutest thing happened. I bent down to pick them up and was grabbing handful by handful. Then I reached for this one pink sock that had little pigs on it, one of Penny's favorite pairs. Luce jumped on my hand, growling. She laid down on top of it and my arm, very clearly not giving up. I think she misses her mama as much as I do. And in her little doggy mind, this was the last bit of her we had, and it must be protected at all costs. So, I bought some stuffing and turned the sock into a little toy for her. She loves it, takes it everywhere; in bed, in the car, even tries to bring it on walks. It made me smile to see her happy again.

5. My barbershop upped it's prices. So, I will be looking for a new one after surgery.

Alright, so there's your life update, back to my epiphany. Warning this is a religious-ish one. God. When you think about it, God is a really wild concept. And I've noticed something about humans; we humanize anything we don't understand. We create correlations to symbols to represent something we can't comprehend on it's natural level. Energy, Life, Love, Death, God. We have fabricated universal images that we use to represent these. With energy and light, we think of lightning bolts and sunbursts. The life we think of green leaves and flowers blooming. Love, we think of hearts. Death is pitch black darkness.

Then there is God. Most of us learned about God as a kid, from whatever adults were in our lives. They gave us easy-to-see images and stories and examples that would stick with us long after we were old enough to know better.

For example, if you grew up Christian, at a young age, you were told something along the lines of "God is this huge man with a beard who lives in the clouds. He is always watching you and loved you enough to give his one and only son for you".

Well, newsflash, humans have been to space, and they didn't see God out the rocket window.

Humans create humanlike images in order to feel a fake sense of comfort in things too complex for us to understand. But here is the thing, if you always break it down, you never see the big picture.

God reaches to every end of infinity. Stop. Take a second to really think about what that means. In every single direction of time and existence, God is there.

Again, people get overwhelmed with larger concepts, so we dumb it down. Infinity, we have programmed our brains to think of it as a size, a destination, a symbol that drunk girls get tattooed on their asses during spring break.

We think of it as a number instead of an existence. We see it as linear, never-ending. And we think of it as being huge. We don't stop to think that the infinite can be intimate. That it can be woven into every cell that has ever existed. Every being, every organism, natural phenomenon, every thought in every single head.

It freaks us out. So, we haven't considered that maybe THAT is God. He isn't some magical being playing a video game that is our lives. That he is not above us, but all around us. He is us. We are him. My thought is: what if God simply is everything.

He isn't the opposition to science, but instead, science is the understanding of him. Even us saying "He" and "Him" are humanizing. He is energy. He is love. He is life and death and everything in between. He is gravity. He is a chemical reaction. Attraction. Repulsion. Friction.

Everything. Everything except time. Time is an entirely manmade construct. God is the only thing truly infinite. Even the word infinite had to be created, which explains why we struggle with it. We scoff at the idea of a God who balances galaxies on his fingertips, worrying about one tiny human soul. I think that's why people, myself included, lose faith. Misunderstanding. They poke holes in the fantasies we were told as children but never take the time to look through them. We use our own vantage point to determine existence. If we don't see it, we don't believe it. We grow our roots stronger and stronger in that idea until we believe it is "physically impossible."

But let me just pop that bubble for a second. What if God controls everything because he IS everything? Think about that for a second. The same entity that concocts hurricanes and changes the seasons, and keeps the planets in rotation, puts a squirrel on your road, so you avoid an accident. The existence that controls all of the oceans, listens to every word you say. He makes the mitochondria of every single cell creating energy. He gives penguins, creatures that in human context are relatively useless. He gives them soulmates. (That's true, look it up.) He devises everything exactly perfectly, down to the last detail.

And we have the nerve to humanize that. To diminish that awesomeness in the name of understanding. And not like a cool skateboard trick awesome, I mean truly awe-inspiring awesomeness. We can't wrap our heads around that. It's unfathomable. But that's kind of the whole fucking point. God is unfathomable to the point even the beings he created can't understand him. That's pretty incredible. Or I am really starting to lose it, and this is all crazy talk. Once again, I'll let you decide, but in the meantime, I'll just keep spilling them as they come to me, until the end of my days, whenever that may be.

Sincerely,
Blown Mind is Better
Than Blown Brains

December 20th

Michael got heartbroken today. His first real heartbreak. They'd been dating for over a year, and it was both of their first loves. Do you remember that? Being young and dumb, getting one sip of love and thinking it was enough to last forever. That somehow, you'd be the lucky one, the one you hear stories about, the love at first sight, all the stars align, high school sweethearts living out the dream that older generations tell us don't exist anymore. That's where he was at. He believed in it wholeheartedly, and because of that, his whole heart got broken.

You know the feeling I am talking about. I don't mean the she-kissed-me-on-the-monkey-bars-and-then-tagged-someone-else-in-freeze tag heartbreak where one good cry, a hug from your mama, and a Capri sun, and you're all better. I mean the real shit. The first time you shatter what you thought was immortal. The first time you feel like your throat is lined with broken glass. The first time a swirling, sucking, a gaping black hole opens in your chest and pulls you into a pit of utter darkness. The fall to your knees, knuckles bleeding, couldn't speak a word other than her name if your life depended on its kind of break. The kind that feels like the end of the world.

But eventually, you learn that the world keeps turning. You're shocked that the sun still rises without her. You are baffled at the rain showers and lightning strikes that you didn't wait for because you had somehow convinced yourself that the love you shared was the contingency of all existence.

I don't think we realize how much of a role love and affection actually play in our lives. I mean, think about it, really think about the last time you loved someone. Didn't they seem to be the center of the universe? Didn't their image find its way into every daydream and plan you had? Didn't you make decisions that affected your life based on their needs as a factor? Didn't you crave only their touch on the bad days? But only theirs. Anyone else you'd punch. Whether we like to admit it or not, I think it's very rare that love isn't a co-star in the play of our life. It's always in the back of our minds. The bottom of our souls and stitched into our beating hearts.

And when you lose it, when it dances its way off the stage and you are left there alone in the spotlight, you want the curtain to drop. You want to restart, to have an intermission to at least process what happens. But as they say, "the show must go on." As painful as the script may be.

But when you are in the middle of it, you don't understand that. Michael doesn't get that right now. He doesn't realize this is one of his defining moments. He doesn't realize this is the story he will someday sit down to tell his kids about when they have their first heartbreak. He doesn't know that this is putting him on the path he's meant for. He doesn't see any of that; all he sees is the pain.

He asked me, how someone can just stop loving you?, How love can just run out like an hourglass you didn't realize was flipped over. And as you of all people are well aware of, I have been having a lot of Big Brain Mr. Poetic Pants moments lately, but this one I actually got to do some good with.

Obviously, I am paraphrasing because I don't remember exactly what I said, but basically, this is the analogy I came up with for him:

Put love in the context of physical pain. If you take away the positives and negatives, characteristically, they are almost identical. So, let's say "true love" blah I hate saying that. Anyway, true love is the equivalent of breaking your arm.

Here's the thing, until you break your arm, you don't know how bad it hurts until you find true love, you don't know what it feels like. Both love and pain require a frame of reference. For example, if you have sprained your arm before, you aren't going to fall for the bruises and love taps of every sweet smile you see. On the flip side, if you have never felt pain in your life, you're going to hear wedding bells with every bump and scrape.

Which is all fine and dandy until you add in the illusion of love. Take a second and think about all the love mirages that have been forced upon us. From the songs on the radio to the princess movies we watched when we were three, the concept of true love has been drilled into our skulls. Subconsciously making us want it more than anything.

This mindset sets our expectations; we go into every relationship thinking, "this is going to break my arm." We exaggerate; we conduct a web of over-romanticized moments, capsizing our feelings, swaying ourselves to believe them. We tell ourselves our arm still hurts. We say it stings because we want it to. But eventually, we can't deny the fact that it's healed. And by the time we get up the courage to walk away, it's a blindside to the other person. They end up broken, and it's our fault because we kept telling them it hurt when we were truly trying to persuade ourselves.

    I don't know if half of that makes sense, but he seemed to get it a little better. It is just so hard to explain to a kid. That there are reasons behind a goodbye. That not everyone is a monster. Granted, there are monsters; there are heartless bastards who play with feelings like voodoo dolls. But most of the people who left us cared enough about us to pretend to love us.

    I tried to tell him that this isn't as bad as he thinks it is. And that the old bullshit saying "when it's it, you just know" isn't bullshit. You'll know when your arm is actually broken. You'll meet someone who will bump into you, and you'll wonder how you've felt pain before. They will ignite every pain cell in your body. And then it will settle. The butterflies stop fluttering, the comfort sets in. All the truths come out. The flame of romance flickers, and you wonder if the pain will stop. But it doesn't. You find the right one, and year after year, your arm will never be the same.

So yeah, it felt like a major Dad moment, but I think I crushed it. He felt better; at least it gave him a little perspective. He'll thank me for it someday. Oh, and he asked me if Penny had broken my arm. I actually laughed out loud. I said if love was physical pain, that woman shattered every bone in me.

                                          Sincerely,
                                        Broken in the Best Way

December 25th

Merry Christmas! Guess what I got you? Go ahead, guess. Yep, another theory! Don't you love it?

I am back at the cabin with my family, not sure if I mentioned that last time. And this year feels different. It's a lot more joyous. The surgery is obviously the biggest buzz going around, and I have gotten a few "how are you hanging in there" head tilts, but for the most part, it's been normal. Like old times, much less of a fishbowl and much more of a zoo exhibit.

I am trying to really enjoy everything, the cookies, the stupid songs I usually put headphones in during, all of it. Everything was going swimmingly until we heard a news report of a fatal car crash. Most of us got sad for a moment but then pushed it out of our minds.

Except for my sister. She's the definition of an empath; she can't just shake things off. Penny was the same way; they always bonded over it. They felt everything as raw and pure as it is. This sank her, and I wasn't quite sure how to pull her out of it. But then I realized maybe she didn't need to be pulled out of it; perhaps she needed someone to wade through it with her. I asked her why things like this get to her so badly.

She explained that it's only partly what actually happened, but more of it could happen to me. I don't know how I found the magic key, but she opened up like she hadn't in years. She spilled all her fears, losing loved ones, death making unwanted appearances when you least expect it. It took me a while to realize she was worried about me.

We then had a conversation that led me to two ideas, and they happened in reverse order, but I think for context, I need to explain it this way.

Firstly, we know we are here to learn lessons; that's the point of life. But consider for a second that your death is your final presentation. Because let's be honest, your death affects your loved ones more than it does you. Their grief is your final exam what they remember you for, how you changed them, how you loved them. Like I said, with legacies, you have very little control of the mark you leave on the world; it is all in the hands of the people who see it. But what if the way you die is actually one of the factors in the mark you leave?

For example, if your friend dies of skin cancer, you're not going to put your pale ass in a tanning bed. If they die of drunk driving, you're going to be more aggressive in taking away the keys from your friends. This is the only thing I can think of to explain why people die in randomly horrible ways, why things like car crashes and cancer and diseases exist. Even murder, granted there is evil in play with that one as well, but the point stands.

It all happens for a reason, which brings us back to our previous conversation, the one about you and hypothetical Julie. You may never get to know the reason, but there is one. So, this is the perspective from the person giving the death presentation. Now flip it.

That brings me to my second realization. If you can't find a reason, be one. If you are sitting there wondering how the hell anything good can come out of so-and-so dying, BE good. Let it be one of your "moments." Let it be a wake-up call. Allow it to change you and push you and break you into the version of you the world needs. Listen to the lessons it's giving you; I promise they are there. You may not realize it for a while, but they are there and as hard as it may be to believe they are necessary.

And I recognize in the suffocating embrace of grief you're not going to believe me. That's okay. You aren't going to be able to think rationally or wonder logically. You aren't going to see any good; you are only going to see the loss. And I understand that, so I'll say this: that's all okay.

You have permission not to believe me. You have clearance to be shallow-minded and self-centered. You have my permission to hate me for saying any of this. You can be mad at me. You can tell me to fuck off because there is no possible way any good could come out of this boiling volcano of shit at the threshold of hell. I am okay with that; I'll be your punching bag; Lord knows you've been mine.

But just remember, there is at least one lesson in every death. And ironically, it is the one that we forget the most: life is short.

We don't know when it's up, but we waste it like it's immortal. Now I am not saying, don't grieve. Absolutely grieve. Cry. Scream. Play their favorite song 400 times in a row. Fuck what the neighbors think. Talk to someone. Sleep in a shirt that smells like them. Never stop missing them and never ever stop loving them. But don't stop living. Don't turn the rest of your life into a shrine for your loss. Live better because of them.

And while we are on the subject, don't feel guilty about it. Don't wipe away the first smile because you are ashamed that you are happy without them. It is okay to feel sadness, but don't live unpack and live in it.

Don't pull a me and waste your life missing her. If you are going to pull a "me," do what I did with The List. Honor them. Live better because of them.

Ah yes, I feel a Mr. Poetic Pants moment coming; let me grab my mustache and monocle:

You owe it to every good person that died too young to live as long and as well as you can.

Boom, another motivational poster for ya. That is basically what I told my sister. That bad things happen, but never haphazardly; there is always a bigger picture. And if you can't find the reason, be the reason. I could tell it really got to her like I was giving her answers she had spent her life looking for. It gave me that warm and fuzzy feeling inside. Even telling you now I have that feeling again. I just don't want you to be so misguided and confused the way I was. Life is worth living no matter who you lose. The only death allowed to kill you is your own.

Sincerely,
Don't Be Like Me

December 31st

Big day tomorrow. Surgery, New Years Day, My birthday, and the one-year anniversary of Lucy saving my life.

Damn, it has been a crazy year, hasn't it? One of the craziest of my life for sure. And I, as always, am going to be honest, I am nervous. I mean, understandably, anytime some dude is going to cut you open, you are going to have worries. But I am not anxious, I am calm. It is weird. Obviously, I am trying to be as positive as I can be, but I just can't shake the feeling that my final presentation is coming soon. The way I have been feeling, the way my mind has been working and figuring out all these things, it just seems like things being tied up in a pretty bow, a clean-cut ending. I just have a feeling it might be.

So just in case, I have spoken my peace to everyone I love. I have had one-on-one with everyone; I've told them what they mean to me, how I see them, how amazing they are. I gave them all little tidbits of advice they can keep in their pockets like a lucky stone and pull it out whenever they need to. I have spoken all of my peace... well, almost. I have just a few more things left to say. To you. Just you.

Firstly, life is always worth living. And it is worth living to the absolute fullest. No matter who you lose, who walks away, what shitstorm rains down on you, it is always worth it. Live the best you fucking can. What is something you have always dreamt of doing but always had an excuse not to? Oh, it's money... oh I have work... oh I have- stop. At the end of your life, the only thing you will have left are memories. Go fucking do it. Go fucking say it. Think about if you died tonight, what have you not said? What words or thoughts would you take to your grave that should have been shouted from the rooftops? It is always worth living.

And with that, it's worth fighting for. Remember we talked about moments? Well, there is one moment that everyone gets. A moment when your head is not only above the waterline, but your feet are firmly in the sand. Your clothes are still wet, but the sun is shining. You get this moment where you feel like you made it. It doesn't mean life is perfect. It means that you are here and you are happy about it.

It's never a big celebration or event. It is a face you love smiling over a plate of nachos. It is a dandelion wish you weren't expecting. You just breathe, and you realize that you're okay. And as bad as things may get, as dark as they may seem, everyone gets that moment. So, promise me, you'll fight for yours. For the love of God, promise me.

Major poetic pants moment, but I just needed to know you knew that. Hopefully, it won't take you as long to figure out as it did for me, because even though the past year has been absolute hell, I would do it all over again. Hell, I would do this whole life over again, it has taught me so much. It taught me the value of moments. About grief, and pain, and love.

Goddamn, has all this taught me about love. Real. True. Vulnerable. Unconditional. Understanding love. To have the ability to open up and share a completely unfiltered version of me with someone. Sharing ideas and beliefs with zero worries of judgment. That is priceless. That kind of love. That shit is strong enough to become your life's purpose. That shit is worth living for. And I have found that... in you.

Yes, you, reading this right now. The one holding this in your hands. Don't get me wrong; Annalise is my best friend, Penny is the love of my life. But the greatest love I have ever had is you. I have felt you through these pages, as I am sure you have felt me. You have listened to my stories, my problems, my life. You empathized with my feelings. Every question I asked you, I heard your answer. I don't know what you look like or where you are. I don't even know who you are, but it doesn't matter. I know you as you have known me. Truly. Unapologetically. You have seen me shattered. You have seen me at peace. You have dealt with my being a dick, and you've listened to the ramblings of Mr. Poetic Pants. And I have known variations of you. Every time you jumped into my world, I glanced into yours. I was with you. I smiled on your good days and sat with you on the bad.

So, with that being said, if this doesn't go as planned. If this is the end...

Actually, scratch that. WHENEVER the end is for me, if there is a snowballs chance in a life after death,

I will do everything I can to be with you. No matter if that is tomorrow or 50 years from now, I will come back to you, I will stay with you long after you have put this on the shelf. Long after you have forgotten me, I will still be with you.

Now, obviously, hopefully, this is just me being dramatic, and I'll be talking to you tomorrow bitching about the hospital jello. But I wanted to tell you that just in case. Life is short and crazy and chaotic, but we always gravitate back to the things that are meant for us; in my case, that was you. So, thank you. Thank you for listening. Thank you for teaching me to believe again. Thank you for being you and being here.

Alright, I have to rest enough sappy shit. But I just wanted you to know; it's you and me. No matter what happens tomorrow. It's you and me. Always. So, one way or another, I'll see you soon.

Sincerely,
William

www.ingramcontent.com/pod-product-compliance
Lightning Source LLC
Chambersburg PA
CBHW061727070526
44583CB00024B/3034